Technology and Literacy in the Twenty-First Century

Studies in Writing & Rhetoric

In 1980 the Conference on College Composition and Communication established the Studies in Writing & Rhetoric (SWR) series as a forum for monograph-length arguments or presentations that engage general compositionists. SWR encourages extended essays or research reports addressing any issue in composition and rhetoric from any theoretical or research perspective as long as the general significance to the field is clear. Previous SWR publications serve as models for prospective authors; in addition, contributors may propose alternate formats and agendas that inform or extend the field's current debates.

SWR is particularly interested in projects that connect the specific research site or theoretical framework to contemporary classroom and institutional contexts of direct concern to compositionists across the nation. Such connections may come from several approaches, including cultural, theoretical, field-based, gendered, historical, and interdisciplinary. SWR especially encourages monographs by scholars early in their careers, by established scholars who wish to share an insight or exhortation with the field, and by scholars of color.

The SWR series editor and editorial board members are committed to working closely with prospective authors and offering significant developmental advice for encouraged manuscripts and prospectuses. Editorships rotate every five years. Prospective authors intending to submit a prospectus during the 1997 to 2002 editorial appointment should obtain submission guidelines from Robert Brooke, SWR editor, University of Nebraska–Lincoln, Department of English, P.O. Box 880337, 202 Andrews Hall, Lincoln, NE 68588-0337.

General inquiries may also be addressed to Sponsoring Editor, Studies in Writing and Rhetoric, Southern Illinois University Press, P.O. Box 3697, Carbondale, IL 62902-3697.

Technology and Literacy in the Twenty-First Century

The Importance of Paying Attention

Cynthia L. Selfe
With a Foreword by Hugh Burns

SOUTHERN ILLINOIS UNIVERSITY PRESS

Carbondale and Edwardsville

Publication partially funded by a subvention grant from The Conference on College Composition and Communication of the National Council of Teachers of English.

Library of Congress Cataloging-in-Publication Data

Selfe, Cynthia L., 1951–
Technology and literacy in the twenty-first century : the importance of paying attention / Cynthia L. Selfe ; with a foreword by Hugh Burns.
    p. cm. — (Studies in writing and rhetoric)
Includes bibliographical references (p.   ) and index.
    1. Computers and literacy—United States. 2. Technological literacy—United States. 3. Literacy—Social aspects—United States. I. Title. II. Series: Studies in writing & rhetoric.
    LC149.5.S45 1999)   99-11478
    371.33′4—dc21   CIP
    ISBN 0-8093-2269-2 (pbk. : alk. paper)

The paper used in this publication meets the minimum requirements of American National Standard for Information Sciences—Permanence of Paper for Printed Library Materials, ANSI Z39.48-1984. ∞

*To the membership and the
leadership of the CCCC,
to the dedicated staff of the National
Council of Teachers of English,
and to all of the talented teachers
of composition, English studies, language
arts, and literacy around the world*

Contents

Foreword: In the Best Modern Way

You may not recognize the name of Cynthia L. Selfe, but to so many of us in the language arts profession, she is a leader of common and uncommon sense. I have known her for over twenty years from our days as graduate students at the University of Texas at Austin. There, we both began to learn something about the possibilities and pitfalls of using technology to teach English. She understands how democracy should work in education and how education must work for democracy. Recently, as chair of the Conference on College Composition and Communication, her leadership made us better than we were, made us appear more unified and collaborative despite our profession's many delightful differences. This book, *Technology and Literacy in the Twenty-First Century: The Importance of Paying Attention*, for me represents both a culmination of Selfe's leadership thus far and a commitment to lead us further still.

Even though these nine chapters raise an ambitious range of cultural, social, and political issues, Selfe writes that this "book was written for teachers of English studies, language arts, and composition." We are her audience because we understand that in the next millennium, technology will make each one of us (1) *a teacher* of data-rich English, (2) *a user* of networked literacy tools, and (3) *a writer and a reader* of digital text. If ubiquitous technology is the reality, then universal humanity and global literacy are the prerequisites.

I first heard Cynthia present a keynote adaptation of this book in April 1998. I was attending the Conference on College Composition and Communication in Chicago. As I made my way up to the front of Palmer House Grand Ballroom to attend her chair's address, I knew I would hear a teacher, a scholar, a writer, an administrator, an editor, a program builder, and a leader. I knew I was also coming to hear my friend whose distinguished career in higher education, as John Dewey might have said, had been "animated by a social spirit in the first place."

I was not alone. I sat among thousands of college composition teachers. That April morning, she challenged our ivory-tower purity and encouraged us to pay attention to matters of literacy and matters of technology in our teaching and in our students' lives. I was not surprised. She had been reminding me to pay attention for over twenty years. Cindy Selfe had helped everyone in that grand ballroom understand technology. Still I thought that some members of that audience might not appreciate how much this one scholar-leader had contributed. I thought some might not realize how firmly anchored her beliefs are—solidly connected to the foundations of rhetorical theory, curriculum development, professional and technical writing practice, and research design. Let me tell you about Cindy.

In 1977, Cindy and I met. We were both graduate students researching James L. Kinneavy's *A Theory of Discourse*. We were guided by scholar-leaders such as Geneva Pilgrim who made us read, Charles R. "Bob" Kline who made us think, Edmund Farrell who made us demonstrate, Maxine Hairston who made us connect, George H. Culp who made us program, and James L. Kinneavy, who made us believe in purposes. Cindy focused her work on the process of writing and the heuristics of expressive discourse; I focused mine on invention and the heuristics of persuasion. Both of us were converts to what was then a radical notion in English departments that one learns to write by writing, that revision is rethinking, that forethought is useful, and that problem solving is recursive. For us, rhetoric was the counterpart of dialectic and knowledge making was not a bad thing. We bonded in that sacred graduate student rite: if you read my data, I shall read your data.

Enter technology, specifically enter the University of Texas at Austin's mainframe electronic computer manufactured by Digital, the DEC 10. I started to write software to generate billions of haiku, to combine sentences in random syntactic styles, to help writers brainstorm, and to help format dissertation margins. If I programmed it, Cindy tried it. If she liked the program, she told me. If she didn't, she told me. She and I learned new words together such as *byte, bit, loop, string, hardwired,* and *modem.* More than sharing data, we were sharing a curiosity about how teachers might really use technology. Those were the early years—but not that long ago. During those hectic years, we both discovered that the digital machine in the humanities garden had potential. That potential, however, could only be realized if the theories we trusted could be designed, developed, tested, and evaluated by writers and by writing teachers. Together, we realized that computer-assisted drill-and-practice tutors would give way to computer-assisted tools for writing. As personal computing exploded on the scene in the 1980s, we realized that personal digital technologies, if well designed and well delivered, would support many literacies. By then, Cindy was helping to build one of this nation's best graduate programs in professional and technical writing at Michigan Technological University. Then I was investigating artificial intelligence applications for technical training for the Air Force.

Soon Selfe's good sense in articulating a teacher's agenda and a technological context for literacy education became the hallmark of her scholarly leadership. In 1982 with Kate Kiefer, and later with Gail Hawisher, she founded and edited *Computers and Composition: An International Journal for Teachers of English.* As Cindy consistently paid attention to the daily demands of teaching composition, a community formed around her—and grew and grew. When the National Council of Teachers of English needed her leadership for the Assembly on Computers in English, she was there. When the Modern Language Association needed her expertise on its Committee on Computers and Emerging Technology, she was there. Now and then, we consulted together and could catch up over dinner at the top of the World Trade Center. Her days then were filled with writing, and soon her vita was full with publications. Let me highlight just a few.

Selfe's *Computers and the Teaching of Writing in American Higher Education, 1979–1994: A History* (Ablex, 1996) with Gail Hawisher, Paul LeBlanc, and Charles Moran invites reflection on the computers and writing community as it emerged. Looking back, the many essays Selfe et al. have collected now form the essential reading list in computers and writing. They are:

> *Literacy, Technology, and Society: Confronting the Issues* (with Gail Hawisher; Prentice Hall, 1997)
>
> *Literacy and Technology* (with Susan Hilligoss; Modern Language Association, 1994)
>
> *Evolving Perspectives on Computers and Composition Studies: Questions for the 1990s* (with Gail Hawisher; National Council of Teachers of English and Computers and Composition Press, 1991)
>
> *Computers and Writing: Theory, Research, and Practice* (with Deborah Holdstein; Modern Language Association, 1990)
>
> *Critical Perspectives on Computers in Composition Instruction* (with Gail Hawisher: Teachers College Press, 1989)

Of course, Selfe's own articles in *College English, College Composition and Communication, Research in the Teaching of English, Journal of Advanced Composition, Technical Communication Quarterly*, and *Written Communication*, among others, give her a right to play Socrates to our Phaedrus.

Her pioneering accomplishments and these numerous publications on technical communications, on technology and literacy, on managing computer-supported writing facilities were honored in 1996 by EDUCOM—the professional association of higher education computing professionals—at their annual convention in Philadelphia. Representing Smith College as the director of educational technology, I watched and applauded as she was presented the first EDUCOM Medal Award for the "effective use of technology in higher education"—the first woman and the first English teacher ever to have received the award.

Now I watched again. Chicago. April 1998. This was the moment in Selfe's professional life when the worlds of life, work, and school collide. Her speech energized me. To paraphrase Yeats in "Among School Children": *Her eyes in momentary wonder stared upon her public crowd. In the best modern way. Questioning.* To use a metaphor from thermodynamics, her speech required, and her text here requires, an audience willing to experience a quantum leap in political energy. Synergistic reminding—that is what Selfe accomplished for me that morning and is sharing again with us in this monograph. Here, friends, she is saying, is the big picture. She is questioning us. If you are not paying attention now, when will you? If not now, when?

Suffice it to say, her analysis of the American social investment in the new literacy agenda is credible in the best modern way. Her challenge for responsible action is passionate in the best modern way. Her case to design and develop an appropriate educational philosophy using technology for literacy's sake is solid. How will this happen? That process, Selfe argues, begins by paying attention. Literacy first. Technology second.

So much political rhetoric these days has to do with improving literacy *in the future.* Certainly, to teach the future means knowing the past, but, Selfe argues, to teach the future means to attend to the present. For Selfe, future action assumes critical attention now. Making computers appear in every classroom—this is a popular political event on campuses. Ribbons are cut. Making critical thinking appear in every classroom, that's another matter. Ropes are strung. Teaching well is risky business. While schoolhouse walls may not tumble down, while browsers may not find exactly what students need to know when students need to know it, while access alone may not empower learning—Selfe is clear that technology is coming and that technological approaches promise new literacy panoramas and new critical perspectives. There is good news. There is bad news.

As you will soon read, Selfe's recommendations require that we have radically rethought our ideas about what schools are and what they should be. She is telling us to be prepared. Know thyself. Know thy theory. Know thy pedagogy. Know thy policy. Know thy practice.

When President Clinton proposes, "purely and simply, that

every single child must have access to a computer," Selfe proposes readiness and critical response. Access? *Do you mean equal?* Pure? *Do you mean political?* Simple? *Do you mean economically?* Every single child? *Do you mean all children?* Pay attention. At the top of her list, not surprising for a chair of a department of humanities, is the capacity for critical thinking. *Questioning. In the best modern way.*

Does policy alone break the cycle of illiteracy, failure, fear, and poverty? Do national goals unattended by state and local resources improve the collective probability for social survival and social excellence? Simple? Hardly, this separating of the technology dancer from the literacy dance.

On April 2, 1998, again in the Palmer House Hilton, nearly one hundred members of the "Fifth C: Computers, Special Interest Group" met to discuss the issues Selfe raised. The facilitators—Eric Crump of the National Council for Teachers of English, Traci Gardner of the Daedalus Group, Cynthia Haynes of the University of Texas at Dallas, and Judi Kirkpatrick of Kapiolani Community College—guided the group discussion. Gardner reminded the audience of Selfe's millennial hypothesis:

> Access to technology is not the liberating or empowering thing that we expect it to be. As composition teachers, deciding whether or not to use technology in our classes is simply not the point—we have to pay attention to technology. When we fail to do so, we share in the responsibility for sustaining and reproducing an unfair system that . . . enacts social violence and ensures continuing illiteracy under the aegis of education.

We formed into groups, and we began paying attention. The teachers present that evening understood technology's potential to transform learning by extending community by using state-of-the-art educational tools. Many were participating in building their campus's technology infrastructure. There was considerable agreement that our colleges and universities—and even our communities—would have universal connectivity and communication. As

to Selfe's lessons, there was also more agreement. National policy
should stimulate, but *paying attention* means guiding and shaping.
Politics happens, but *paying attention* means never having to acqui-
esce ethically or economically. Technology disappears, but *paying
attention* means not until humanity appears.

As to the consequences of technology in literacy education,
the conversations continued until dawn—and beyond. Does technology integration alone enable students to be more effective writers and more productive world citizens? Does the use of technology
really bring the world into the classroom, breaking down barriers of ethnocentricity and prejudice? Does distance learning and
teleconferencing truly provide an equitable means of connecting
students across geographical, political, and cultural boundaries?
Again, questioning.

Some guidelines emerged. One group boldly wrote their own
credo:

WE BELIEVE . . .
That as educators we need to get up to speed so that we can
teach others;
That we need professional development—hardware and
software training, critical consciousness of technology—
what it does to, and for, people;
That we need professional development in the integration
of technology into our teaching;
That our institutions' budgets should spend twice what they
spend on equipment and depreciation on training and
support staff;
That funding for technology must come from new
sources—not at the expense of teaching staff, school
lunch programs, or any social support services.

Another group drafted a "Sense of the House Resolution" for Satur-
day morning's business meeting.

Whereas Cynthia Selfe, chair of CCCC [Conference on
College Composition and Communication], issued a call

to action in her keynote address on Thursday, urging us to take a professional stand on a variety of technological issues affecting access, funding, and literacy practices,

Be it resolved that CCCC encourage the Committee on Computers in Composition and Communication to draft guidelines and suggest standards for creating, funding, supporting, and assessing technology initiatives in composition and literacy instruction, and that these guidelines and standards inform the drafting of a CCCC statement on these issues.

Many still are paying attention on the road and on the World Wide Web. At a recent fall forum on "Women, Minorities, and Computing Technology" at my own university, Texas Woman's University, Cynthia Haynes spoke to us of the nuances of access:

I find that the question of access has some invisible nuances that Cindy [Selfe] latches on to as she urges our field to go beyond teaching with technology and begin to critically pay attention. But there is one nuance that nags at me whenever I try to "speak for" or "represent" the views of any underrepresented group, and I credit Gayatri Spivak for calling my attention to it. She claims that we must always "pay attention to our own subjective investment in the narratives that we produce." Selfe is calling for our field to pay attention to its own subjective investment in the narratives it produces.

Paying attention is a subjective investment. Paying attention begins the narrative. Paying attention is production. So this foreword shall conclude.

Selfe has started a national conversation. My "animated social spirit in the first place" friend and colleague has renewed our search to use technology wisely in our profession—but also in yours. An energetic scholar, her visionary leadership has established a national agenda for the theory and practice of technical, literate, professional, humane, and expressive discourse. An enthusiastic teacher, her lessons establish that there is still much to learn and to do. With careful attention paid to technology, however, the twenty-first-century educator she envisions is one who shall enable a literacy of the people, for the people, and by the people.

What will happen to the schools of tomorrow? More important, what will happen to the students of tomorrow? Time will tell. But because we paid attention, because we learned to love the complications, because we defined how technology was inextricably linked to literacy, we were ready. We were better prepared to instruct, to move, to please, and to learn.

The moment you finish reading *Technology and Literacy in the Twenty-First Century: The Importance of Paying Attention*, just remember one face among the sea of faces you have taught. Then imagine a face of one student you will teach tomorrow.

The expressions on those two faces will tell the tale.

Did you pay attention? Did you question?

Questioning? In the best modern way?

Hugh Burns

Introduction: Paying Attention to the Technology-Literacy Linkage

This is a book written for teachers of English studies, language arts, and composition. It is about literacy, but it is also about technology. On the following pages, I explore the complex linkage between technology and literacy that has come to characterize American culture and its public educational system at the end of the twentieth century. To provide a specific case study of this complex cultural formation, I focus a great deal of the discussion on the Technology Literacy Challenge, a federal literacy project begun in 1996 that has redefined literacy and the practices recognized as constituting literate behavior in America.

Most important, I try to identify the effects of this new literacy agenda, focusing specifically on the serious and shameful inequities it continues to generate within our culture and the public education system, including the continuing presence of racism, poverty, and illiteracy. The following chapters describe how the national project to expand technological literacy came about, what effects it has yielded, why the American public has supported this project, and how teachers have contributed to this project.

My goal is to make teachers aware of this new literacy agenda and to suggest how they might act in productive ways to influence its shape and future direction, both in the classroom and in the community. This awareness is an integral part of educators' larger professional responsibility to understand the way in which our culture thinks about and values literacy. Perhaps even more important, this awareness is part of our ethical responsibility to understand how literacy and literacy instruction directly and continually affects the lived experiences of the individuals and families with whom we come into contact as teachers.

This book is organized in three parts. In part one, I outline the parameters of the contemporary push for technological literacy in the United States and the direct challenges that this social project poses for English composition, language arts, and literacy educators:

- Although the push for technological literacy is supposed to benefit all Americans, it has instead supported, and perhaps exacerbated, inequities in American culture.

- Because the push for technological literacy focuses on one officially sanctioned form of literacy, it encourages citizens to discount the complexities of literacy education and the importance of multiple literacies within our culture.

- The push for technological literacy operates in an intellectual context of either/or representations of technology, with neither side accurately portraying the complexities associated with technological literacies practices and values.

In short, the contemporary project to expand technological literacy in America has not lived up to our cultural expectations. Moreover, this project has enjoyed only limited success in improving our country's educational efforts.

These failings are consequences, in part, of a definition of *technological literacy* that is both limited and incomplete. The prevailing cultural understanding of the term as simple *competence with computers* serves to misdirect the energy put into the national project to expand technological literacy—limiting the effectiveness of literacy instruction as it occurs within schools and homes in this country, and hindering efforts to formulate increasingly complex and robust accounts of technological literacy. Educators need to address this misdirection at several levels before they can contribute to more accurate and complete understandings of technological literacy.

In part two, I try to show that the misdirection associated with the current definition of technological literacy is not a simple matter; rather, it is motivated and encouraged by a related cluster of cultural forces that serve both political and economic ends. Teachers who hope to address some of the inequities associated with technological literacy need to understand that the existing situation grows out of a complexly related cluster of overlapping cultural forces:

- government initiatives designed to ensure the vitality of American industrial and political efforts at home and abroad,
- educators—including English and language arts teachers—seeking to prepare students at all levels for an increasingly technological society in the twenty-first century,
- private sector businesses seeking to improve profits and markets by creating an ongoing demand for increasingly sophisticated computer goods,
- parents seeking to improve their children's future prospects by providing home technologies and early training in technological literacy.

In their contemporary configuration, these articulated forces work together to create an agenda for technological literacy that requires the investment of all segments of American society—families, schools, private sector, government. This agenda sustains an increasingly vigorous domestic computer sector and helps create and extend the world market for American technology.

This configuration is coherent, based on shared commonsense understandings, and deeply sedimented in American culture. And given the potency of the configuration, it is no wonder that government, education, business, and families are supporting each other in defining and pursuing the new agenda of technological literacy. But this present configuration is also partial and problematic. It disguises the fact that technology is *not* available to everyone in this country or to every student in our schools. It directs our attention away from the realization that, in America, technology supports social divisions along race, class, and gender. It keeps us from fully understanding the complexities of literacy values and practices and from defining literacy instruction in ways that could help address some of these problems. In sum, the real work facing teachers involves transforming our current limited discussions about technological literacy into more fully informed debates acknowledging the complex relationships between technology, literacy, education, power, economic conditions, and political goals. It is only after we have undertaken this work that we can make productive change.

I analyze the contributions of four cultural forces—government, education, business, and parents—to the existing configuration of technological literacy. I will claim that this combination of forces constitutes an ideological complex based on a commonsense belief in technology. This belief system masks some very real effects of technological literacy from our national consciousness. I explain how the current cultural placement of technological literacy within the educational system commits us, as educators, to supporting the limited goals associated with technological literacy and implicates us in the social inequities associated with this formation. I analyze the problem defined in the first part of this book and explore the cultural forces that contribute to it.

Part three focuses on the lessons that the current situation can yield for literacy educators and the ways in which teachers can shape and direct their efforts in connection with the new literacy agenda. This section details the lessons that educators can relearn about literacy, specifically by paying attention to technology and the ways in which technology is currently being approached in our culture at large and within the public schooling system. This final section also suggests sites within which teachers of literacy can shape the relationship between technology and literacy in increasingly active and productive ways.

Our professional recognition that computers can potentially provide support for educational efforts is only the barest of starting points. This understanding has brought us only to the point of using computers but not to the much more important point of thinking about what we are doing and trying to understand the broader social implications of our actions. At the beginning of the twenty-first century, it has become increasingly clear that teachers of composition, English studies, and language arts also have two much larger and more complicated obligations: first, paying attention to how technology is now inextricably linked to literacy and literacy education in this country; and, second, helping colleagues, students, administrators, politicians, and other Americans use their increasingly critical and productive perspective on technological literacy to make productive social change.

With these two goals in mind—paying attention and working toward productive change—and with great respect for the powerful social and intellectual force that teachers of literacy collectively represent, I begin and end this book.

Part One

A New Literacy Agenda
and Its Challenges

1 / Literacy and Technology Linked: The National Project to Expand Technological Literacy

[T]he NII can transform the lives of the American people—ameliorating the constraints of geography, disability, and economic status—giving all Americans a fair opportunity to go as far as their talents and ambitions will take them. . . . The . . . NII will "create as much as $300 billion annually in new sales across a range of industries." The . . . NII would increase the GDP by $194 billion . . . [and add] $321 billion to the GNP by the year 2007, and increase productivity by 20 to 40 percent. (*National Information Infrastructure* 4)

Technological literacy—meaning computer skills and the ability to use computers and other technology to improve learning, productivity, and performance—has become as fundamental to a person's ability to navigate through society as traditional skills like reading, writing, and arithmetic. . . .

[O]n February 15, 1996, President Clinton and Vice President Gore announced the Technology Literacy Challenge, envisioning a twenty-first century where all students are technologically literate. The challenge was put before the nation as a whole, with responsibility shared by local communities, states, the private sector, educators, local communities, parents, the federal government, and others. (*Getting America's Students Ready* 5)

Literacy's Changing Agenda

Literacy alone is no longer our business. Literacy and technology are. Or so they must become.

3

Who would have predicted that English studies, composition, and language arts teachers at the beginning of the twenty-first century would be so desperately needed? And needed not only for our expertise with language and literacy studies but for the attention we pay—as humanist scholars, teachers, and citizens—to the complex set of social, political, educational, and economic challenges associated with technology. But here we are.

Increasingly, literacy educators have recognized that Americans need help as they prepare to face the technological challenges of the next century, that the primary battles of the computer revolution are far from over. In print, television, and on-line media and thus in our country's collectively structured public imagination, significant battles are still being waged over computer technology and its relationship to various social agendas, both dominant and minority, within the United States. Americans continue to struggle with the government's responsibility for providing access to technology and with the corporate sector's responsibility for remaining competitive in an increasingly technological global market. Many wrestle as well with the role of the country's educational system in producing an informed citizenry that knows how to use computers and with the responsibility that parents have for providing children with computer support at home. Many are confronted with the changing nature of intellectual property in electronic environments, changing expectations about privacy in personal e-mail exchanges, and changing understandings of what it means to be a writer or a reader or even a person in cyber environments. And these questions represent only a few of the issues that technology raises.

These struggles—and the public debates that characterize them—are significant because they help shape America's ongoing relationship with technology, the ways in which citizens think of human agency within this relationship, and the ways in which Americans put computers to work in the service of those social projects that are most important to the nation's commonweal.

Nowhere are such struggles and debates rendered in more complex terms—and nowhere are they more influential—than in the field of literacy: composition, language arts, and rhetoric. For teachers, literacy instruction is now inextricably linked with technology. Moreover, since 1993, an official national project to expand technological literacy has been launched in America's schools, homes, and workplaces, changing the ways in which both literacy educators and the publics they serve think about, value, and practice literacy. This national project bears directly on the work we do as literacy specialists. Technology has become part of our responsibility, whether we like it or not.

My purpose is to convince teachers of English studies, composition, and language arts that we must turn our attention to technology and its general relationship to literacy education. On the specific project to expand technological literacy, we must bring to bear the collective strength of our profession and the broad range of intellectual skills we can muster as a diverse set of individuals. The price we pay for ignoring this situation is the clear and shameful recognition that we have failed students, failed as humanists, and failed to establish an ethical foundation for future educational efforts in this country.

The Challenges Associated with the New Agenda

If the increasingly strong cultural link between technology and literacy is the general area of concern in this book, the specific case study of this cultural formation is the current national project to expand technological literacy, officially identified as the Technology Literacy Challenge by the Clinton administration (*Getting America's Students Ready*). This project aims to create a citizenry comfortable in using computers not only for the purposes of calculating, programming, and designing but also for the purposes of reading, writing, and communicating. It is an excellent case study of a national literacy project because of the tremendous scope, significance, currency, and cost associated with such goals.

According to its sponsors, this large-scale literacy project will offer all Americans equal access to an education rich in opportunities to use and learn about technology. With such an education, the project's sponsors claim, graduates will be qualified for high-paying high-tech jobs and thus have the means of achieving upward social mobility and economic prosperity within our increasingly technological culture.

To achieve this goal, American schools must help "all of our children to become technologically literate" by teaching them to use communication technologies, specifically computers, in the practice of reading and writing effectively. The deadline for creating such a citizenry—one that understands literacy practices in terms of technological contexts—is "early in the 21st century" (*Getting America's Students Ready* 3).

But if the project to expand technological literacy has been justified as a means of achieving positive social change and new opportunity, to date it has failed to yield the significant social progress or productive changes that many people have come to hope for. Indeed, in the American school system as a whole, and in the culture that this system reflects, computers continue to be distributed differentially along the related axes of race and socioeconomic status, and this distribution contributes to ongoing patterns of racism and to the continuation of poverty.

It is a fact, for instance, that schools primarily serving students of color and poor students continue to have access to fewer computers and to less sophisticated computer equipment than do schools primarily serving more affluent students or white students. And it is a fact that schools primarily serving students of color and poor students continue to have less access to the Internet, to multimedia equipment, to CD-ROM equipment, to local area networks, and to videodisk technology than do schools primarily serving more affluent and white students (Coley, Crandler, and Engle 3).

These data, which are profoundly disturbing, become all the more problematic if we trace the extended effects of the technology-literacy link into the country's workplaces and homes. There, too, the latest census figures indicate, the link is strongly correlated to both race and socioeconomic status. Black employees are less likely than white employees to use a range of computer applications in their workplace environments. Employees who have not graduated from high school are less likely to use a range of computer applications than are employees who have a high school diploma or have some college experience. And families of color and families with low incomes are less likely to own and use computers than white families and families with higher incomes (see *Condition of Education 1997* 212; *Digest of Education Statistics 1996* 458–59; *Getting America's Students Ready* 36). In other words, the poorer and the less educated Americans are in this country—both of which conditions continue to be closely correlated with race—the less likely they are to have access to computers and to high-paying hightech jobs.

In these terms, then, the national project to expand technological literacy has not resulted in a better life or more democratic opportunities or an enriched educational experience for all Americans, as most of us might wish. Rather, it has served to improve the education only for some Americans. This specific project—and the more general social forces and formations that sustain it—substitutes a value on competition and consumerism for a commitment to equal opportunity, democratic cooperation, and a public education that serves the common good of this country's peoples.

In a formulation that literacy educators will feel most keenly, the project to expand technological literacy implicates literacy and illiteracy—in their officially defined forms—in the continued reproduction of poverty and racism. And it implicates teachers as well, despite our best intentions.

The Social and Educational Effects of the New Agenda

An honest examination of the situation surrounding the project to expand technological literacy suggests that these two complex cultural formations, technology and literacy, have become linked in ways that exacerbate current educational and social inequities in the United States rather than addressing them productively. Such an examination encourages teachers to admit, moreover, that we may be partially responsible for this bad, even shameful, situation.

The project to expand technological literacy has not clearly bene-fited all Americans in ways that would warrant its expense, despite the size and scope of the efforts that have been undertaken thus far. Of course, it is true that some Americans have benefited. Cer-tainly the computer industry has grown during the 1990s (see *Eco-nomic Report of the President*; Freeman; Goodman; McConnell; Warnke). And the project has created some changes in the na-tion's schools. As of 1994, for example, 68.3 percent of fourth-grade students, 82.3 percent of eighth graders, and 86.9 percent of high school juniors were writing stories or papers on computers (*Condi-tion of Education 1997* 56), and 43 percent of fourth-grade teachers and 17 percent of eighth-grade teachers reported using computers to teach reading (Coley, Crandler, and Engle 29). Today, 98 percent of all schools own at least some computers, and the ratio of comput-ers to students, at 1:10, is at an all-time low (Coley, Crandler, and Engle 3). In some cases, these changes have resulted in educational approaches that are increasingly engaging and rewarding for stu-dents, that reduce some of the unnecessary labor associated with writing (e.g., recopying text in the effort of revising, photocopy-ing, or reproducing copies of texts in order to share them with oth-ers), or that alleviate the workload of teachers (see *Getting America's Students Ready*; Hawisher et al.; Handa; Selfe and Hilligoss; and Strickland).

However, the national project to expand technological literacy has also failed to yield some of the expected reforms. For example, although it has resulted in some surface changes in how literacy is practiced and what Americans consider literate behaviors, it has not resulted in an improved life for all citizens—especially poor stu-dents or students of color who, within this country's educational system, continue to have less access to technology (Coley, Crandler, and Engle) and who suffer from a higher incidence of educational failure than wealthier students and white students (*Condition of Education 1997* 212).

Indeed, although the project has been justified as a means of achieving positive social change and new opportunity, it actually serves a fundamentally conservative role. This project is linked to the continued reproduction of the following familiar social elements:

- A "literate" segment of society—composed of individuals with relatively high levels of technological literacy skills, distributed generally along existing axes of wealth and privilege—who will yield the country's leaders and productively employed workers.

- An "illiterate" segment of society—so labeled because individuals within it fail to acquire sufficient skills in technological literacy—on whom our culture relies for the most undesirable tasks in our society and who will continue to suffer disproportionately from persistent social problems like poverty and crime.

- A stable citizenry that continues to be sorted hierarchically into social subgroups based systematically on links between race and class and the related effects of differential literacy levels, educational opportunities, health environments, and access to technology.

- A citizenry that believes in the potential of high-tech literacy instruction to make lives better, to ensure progress, and to provide a route to economic prosperity. Unfortunately, the very hopefulness of this group generally blinds them to the important connection between the literacy instruction in our existing educational system and that system's role in reproducing persistent social problems.

Our Professional Responsibility

Surprisingly, given its broad cultural significance, this extensive national project has received little or no focused attention or comprehensive response from literacy teachers and scholars. In part, literacy issues have enjoyed such a low profile in discussions of this national project because teachers remain comfortable with the culture's traditional separation of arts and technology (see Snow; and Latour, Preface) as it has served to structure the responsibilities of

English studies professionals. This conventional separation, after all, has allowed us to use technology in our classrooms while generally absolving ourselves from the responsibility for planning for technology, thinking critically about technology, systematically assessing the value of technology, and making the difficult decisions associated with who pays for and has access to technology (see Hawisher and Selfe 1993; R. Selfe; Selfe and Selfe).

Even recognizing this historically determined set of attitudes, however, it is an understatement to say that literacy educators have failed to recognize the project to expand technological literacy as a coherent nationally funded venture. Indeed, teachers have not responded in any comprehensive or systematic fashion to this project, nor have the professional organizations that represent them demanded any involvement in shaping its goals, even though all teachers have been affected by it.

What makes this decided lack of professional involvement most disturbing is the increasing recognition that the claims associated with this large-scale literacy project have not been borne out. Our profession's reluctance to engage in focused ways with such a significant national effort is both disappointing and problematic. We cannot responsibly afford to maintain our current disinterested profile much longer without engaging in a willful ignorance that yields serious consequences.

What Is Technological Literacy?

In this book, readers will encounter two definitions of technological literacy. These definitions overlap, but they also differ.

The first definition is associated specifically with the national project to expand technological literacy and is identified in the 1996 federal publication *Getting America's Students Ready for the Twenty-First Century*:

> [Technological literacy involves] computer skills and the ability to use computers and other technology to improve learning, productivity, and performance. (5)

It is clear, however, that this specific—and, in some, senses, more narrow—functional definition, like the national project to expand technological literacy, grows out of a broader cultural link between technology and literacy. And this broader link—characterized by a related set of social values, formations, and activities—suggests the need for a second definition of technological literacy as a cultural phenomenon, one that includes cultural dimensions, incorporating what Brian Street identifies as both literacy "events" and literacy "practices" (2).

In this context, the second definition of technological literacy that this book offers (and, indeed, focuses on) refers not only to what is often called "computer literacy," that is, people's functional understanding of what computers are and how they are used, or their basic familiarity with the mechanical skills of keyboarding, storing information, and retrieving it. Rather, *technological literacy* refers to a complex set of socially and culturally situated values, practices, and skills involved in operating linguistically within the context of electronic environments, including reading, writing, and communicating. The term further refers to the linking of technology and literacy at fundamental levels of both conception and social practice. In this context, technological literacy refers to social and cultural contexts for discourse and communication, as well as the social and linguistic products and practices of communication and the ways in which electronic communication environments have become essential parts of our cultural understanding of what it means to be literate.

At the level of literacy events, this second definition of technological literacy refers to the events that involve reading, writing, and communicating within computer-based environments, all of which have come to be socially identified as literate activities. These include understanding and valuing the uses of common computer applications for generating, organizing, manipulating, researching, producing, and distributing information, discourse, and texts (print, still graphics, moving images); and using such tools as databases, word-processing packages, multimedia production packages, e-mail, listserv software, bulletin boards, and graphics and line-art packages. At this level, the term *technological literacy* also refers to the activities associated with navigating on-line communication environments such as the World Wide Web (WWW), the Internet, activities that require, for example, the use of browsers and search engines in order to locate information and engage in on-line conversations.

This second definition of technological literacy, however, also operates at the level of literacy practices. These practices, when examined within the context of a larger social fabric, as literacy scholars such as Street and Gee both point out, reveal robustly defined cultural understandings of the term *literacy* as they are constructed by individuals and groups in specific social settings. When practices of technological literacy are studied closely, they reveal complex sets of cultural beliefs and values that influence—and are influenced by—collective, individual, and historical understandings of what it means to read, write, make meaning, and communicate via computers and within on-line environments.

Cultural values, which are often deeply "sedimented," to use Anthony Giddens's term (22) in history and practice, help determine why some technological literacy skills and practices are associated with this country's official system of literacy and literacy education (as represented in more regulated sites such as school standards and curricula, government documents on education and educational programs, public criteria for the hiring of corporate employees, or educational software products published for home tutoring use) and other practices—in contrast, with a system of nonofficial technological literacy (e.g., as represented in less regulated sites on the WWW, in homes, and in computer games). Given this social and cultural context, those technological literacy skills and practices associated with official efforts are generally considered useful and appropriate (e.g., using the WWW to do research for a project assigned in the workplace, using an e-mail list to communicate with people from other cultures or to practice a skill in another language as assigned in a schooling context, or using a graphics package to illustrate a formal report to a local government representative); and those technological literacy activities associated with nonofficial situations and settings are often considered to be either problematic (e.g., frequenting WWW chatrooms predominated by marginal social groups, cruising the web for pornographic pictures, using the Internet to find recipes for designer drugs, using a web site to join a cult) or outside the official realm of technological literacy altogether (e.g., using an ATM machine, playing a handheld video game, programming a VCR).

Our culture's understanding of official literacy events and practices is shaped by complexly related social formations that function within historical, economic, political, and ideological contexts. Government values on control, competition, and research, for instance, influenced technological literacy practices on the original ARPANET and continue to do so on the National Information Infrastructure (NII). These communication environments first supported government-sponsored military research and, later, corporate research and communication, educational research activities, the distribution of information to citizens, and the provision of citizen-based input to elected officials. Related to the social formation of the state, moreover, are those formations associated with capitalism, including the corporate and industrial sectors. And these sectors, too, contribute to a collective cultural understanding of the official skills that make up technological literacy.

Many corporate literacy practices and values, for example, are determined within the regulating environments of state or federal legislation, government grant programs, or military contracts. Corporate-sponsored projects necessitating the use of the NII, the WWW, or in-house intranets, for instance, often place a high value on the efficiency of communication. In such environments, employees learn to value the speed of e-mail exchanges, the ability to distribute information quickly and widely, and the transactional functions of language. Within the daily operations of the workplace, employees also come to understand that some computer tools and activities are seen as more useful, more focused on corporate outcomes, more productive—and hence more official—than others. Among these might be the use of database tools to enhance the efficient structuring of information within a corporate setting, the use of report-generation and archiving systems to contribute to the efficient production and control of information in an organization, and the use of computer-supported group decision-making packages to solve problems efficiently. Within such contexts, a collective sense of official literacy becomes part of a system that serves to further regulate and control employees' literacy practices in various ways and at various levels with the goal of improving performance and reducing operating costs (see Zuboff; Duin and Hansen; Johnson-Eilola and Selber).

Government and corporate values and practices, moreover, help shape the official programs of technological literacy that the American educational system offers to students. Most schools, for example, now recognize an obligation to teach transactional and functional communication practices within electronic environments. The goal is to provide students with marketable skills and to produce a technologically skilled citizenry that can contribute to the national commonweal and to a healthy economy based on the production of increasingly sophisticated technological products and services. Such goals directly inform official versions of technological literacy and are explicitly codified within the standards documents of various professional organizations and the performance frameworks of state educational systems. In the case of technological literacy, both the NCTE *Standards for the English Language Arts* and the *Michigan Curriculum Framework*, for example, mention the need for a computer-literate citizenry.

Finally, the technological literacy practices and skills characterizing official schooling environments often affect technological literacy practices at home (e.g., the use of a home computer and the WWW to complete homework assignments or to practice approved literacy skills) and shape corporate practices (e.g., the design and marketing of educational software packages and hardware products for use on home computers).

Our culture's understanding of unofficial technological literacy practices are generally associated with less regulated—or less overtly regulated—aspects of citizens' lives at home in informal social groups. For example, unofficial technological literacy practices and values are shaped by individuals' access to electronic entertainment and leisure equipment (e.g., electronic games, programmable VCRs and coffee makers, electronic kiosks in shopping malls). Unofficial literacy practices and values are also shaped by individuals' participation in self-selected discussions (e.g., on-line discussions on golf tips, religious cults, raising guppies, designer drugs, ways to avoid paying taxes, or homeopathic remedies) and by their association with informal social groups that use computers (e.g., gay teens who meet on-line, cooking clubs that rely on programmable breadmakers, students who exchange pirated software without paying commercial vendors, friends who get together to play games.).

The Social and Financial Costs of the New Literacy Agenda

The broadly distributed costs of the general link between literacy and technology, manifested in both social and financial terms, are difficult to assess because they affect so many areas of American life (e.g., the costs associated with using computers in schools, developing infrastructure for the Internet, conducting computer research in technology-based industries, making computers available in public libraries) and because, in each venue, these costs must be figured at numerous levels and in different ways (e.g., the costs to individuals, organizations, corporations, communities, states, and nations). Literacy educators can derive a more concrete sense of such costs, however, from the specific case study of the national project to expand technological literacy.

In financial terms, for example, this project has required the collective investment of federal and state governments, funding from the corporate sector, significant commitments from already strapped educational budgets, and direct financial support from individual families across the nation. And this funding has been distributed in many ways.

By 1993, for instance, the general costs of upgrading the NII—the national computer network designed to serve as the foundation for technological literacy practices—were already estimated at $1–2 billion annually (*National Information Infrastructure* 6). And expenditures projected for the specific national project to expand technological literacy indicate that this particular literacy project may run up to $109 billion—averaging either $11 billion annually for a decade or between $10 and $20 billion annually for five years—from various sources at the national, state, and local levels (*Getting America's Students Ready* 6).

Where has this money come from, and where has it gone? As Todd Oppenheimer notes:

> New Jersey cut state aid to a number of school districts this past year and then spent $10 million on classroom computers. In Union City, California, a single school district is spending $27 million to buy new gear for a mere eleven schools. (46)

Secretary of Education Richard Riley, in *Getting America's Students Ready* (60–68), lists other funded projects from various states, including the following items:

California	$279 million (one time, state board) for "instructional technology, deferred maintenance, technology."
	$13.5 million (state board) for educational technology.
	$10 million (state budget) to "refurbish and update used or donated computers."
	$100 million (one year, governor) for "educational technology."
	$35 million (Pacific Telesis) for rate overcharges.
Delaware	$30 million (state, three years) to fund "infrastructure initiative."
District of Columbia	$9 million for "hardware and software purchases."

Idaho	$10.4 million (Idaho Educational Technology Initiative) for "technology in the classroom."
Maine	$15 million (governor) to "establish a distance-learning network."
Montana	$2.56 million (NSF) to support "SummitNet."
	$100,000 (state) "for technology."
Texas	$150 million (state, Telecommunications Infrastructure Fund)
	$30/student (state) for "purchasing electronic textbooks or technological equipment . . . , training educational personnel directly involved in student learning, . . . access to technological equipment."
Wisconsin	$10 million (state) for "improved access to advanced telecommunications and distance education technologies," with 24 percent local match required.

In comparison to the federal funding for other literacy and education projects, these amounts are staggering. The 1999 budget that President Clinton sent to Congress for the Department of Education, for example, requested $721 million of direct federal funding for educational technology, but less than half of that amount, $260 million, for the American Reads Challenge and less than one-tenth of that amount, $67 million, for Teacher Recruitment and Preparation ("President Clinton Sends 1999 Education Budget to Congress" 3).

Even more important than these financial expenditures, however, is America's moral and social investment in literacy education. As Graff, Olson, Street, Gee, and other scholars point out, literacy has historically been considered "the most significant distinguishing feature of a civilized man and a civilized society" and illiteracy has been understood as a condition that carries with it the most "dreadful social and personal consequences" (David Olson, qtd. in Graff 1987, 2). We have come to understand that cultural definitions of literacy have had such import as social constructs because of the potent "normative assumptions and expectations" (Graff 1987, 3) associated with them. The definition of literacy determines not only who will succeed in our culture—and the criteria for such success—but also who will fail. On a pragmatic level, definitions of literacy serve as triggers, or requirements, for other socially determined systems of support. Literacy levels have been used to determine state allocations and eligibility for federal assistance, access to further educational opportunities, employment qualifications, and social assistance. Citizens who can demonstrate sufficient levels of official literacy can obtain a driver's license, apply for a home loan, seek financial support for higher education, and apply for a higher-paying job. Citizens who cannot demonstrate such skills may be unable to accomplish many of these things within the social systems we now have in place. Through these mechanisms, definitions of literacy play a significant role in creating and maintaining a cohesive hegemonic system in the United States that affects every citizen's chances for success.

In terms of our case study examination, the public discourse surrounding the current national project to expand technological literacy—as expressed in the language of state and federal legislation, official educational standards documents, reports from governmental agencies, and news articles—has already figured significantly in determining who is perceived as literate and illiterate in this country. Language that links literacy practices to technological environments, for instance, now directly influences whether children are perceived as ready for preschool in Maine (Blom), whether students fulfill eighth-grade performance standards in Michigan (*Michigan Curriculum Framework*), and whether graduates can meet entry-level job requirements in Florida and California (Geewax; "Tearing U.S. Apart"; Nax).

Brian Street explains the general cultural importance of such discursive phenomenon by pointing out that national and social values are made manifest in—and clearly shape—official definitions of literacy. As he notes, the rhetoric associated with large-scale literacy programs not only draws "public attention to literacy" in particular ways and serves to encourage "financial and organizational resources" (13). It does so along the axes of existing power formations in a society, often following all-too-familiar class patterns, for instance, or racial patterns. For these reasons, Street explains further, large-scale literacy projects often serve not to change a society's educational efforts for the better but, rather, to reproduce stereotypical patterns of responding or failing to respond to individuals from nondominant groups such as the poor or people of color.

Moreover, as Street cautions, the public discourse associated with large-scale literacy programs, while revelatory in terms of national values, can also be misleading in terms of actual outcomes. It often implies erroneously, for example, that the acquisition of literacy leads, autonomously and directly, to improved "job prospects, social mobility, and personal achievement" (17) and that individuals who remain "illiterate" in terms of officially defined skills lack either the cognitive ability or the personal discipline to succeed. "The reality," Street reminds us, "is more complex" and "harder to face politically."

> Recent studies have shown, for instance, that when it comes to job acquisition, the level of literacy is less important than issues of class, gender, and ethnicity; lack of literacy is more likely to be a symptom of poverty and deprivation than a cause (Graff 1979). . . . Governments have a tendency to blame the victims . . . and "illiteracy" is one convenient way of shifting debate away from the lack of jobs and onto people's own supposed lack of fitness for work. (18)

Street's warnings reinforce the moral and ethical obligations that responsible literacy educators and citizens have in connection with the current national project to expand technological literacy. The ways in which we define literacy in state and federal documents; the literacy practices we support and teach in schools; the official literacy values that we recognize and inculcate as a culture; citizens' chances for jobs, social mobility, and prosperity in this country—all of these are at stake in the current national project, and they are therefore among our professional responsibilities to address.

The import of the national project to expand technological literacy, then, far exceeds the relatively limited impact such an effort will have on the professional efforts of literacy educators, national, state, and local budgets, or school curricula. Rather, it affects the future of all citizens within our democratically conceived society and the opportunities they perceive as their own. For these reasons, we should all think about where we are headed in terms of technological literacy—and why.

The costs associated with the project to expand technological literacy have a basis in family life as well. Parents and families, for example, continue to be charged with the role of preparing their children for the literacy practices that they will encounter in the educational system. In the case of the current project to expand technological literacy, such a task entails supporting children with technology at home. In 1996, for example, Eric Blom reported that "between one-third and one-half of the nation's preschool-age children now have some computer experience." For parents, adapting to such changes may be difficult, in part because many adults raised in the print generation do not possess the skills that students will need to practice in computer-based literacy environments. Indeed, if Margaret Mead is correct, our culture may be changing so rapidly that adults raised in the twentieth century may be incapable of educating children for the world of the twenty-first century.

The project to expand technological literacy has additional implications for parents. Computers are expensive. Americans purchased more than 9.5 million home computers in 1995, making PCs a fixture in approximately 39 percent of U.S. households. By the year 2000, Freeman estimates, 60–65 percent of American households will own computers. On-line service providers, educational software, and computer literacy classes also represent significant costs.

Given such facts, it is not surprising that more children from middle- and high-income households had at-home access to a computer between 1984 and 1993 (from 10.8 to 23.7 percent and from

26.1 to 55.3 percent, respectively, for students reporting in grades 7–12) than did children from low-income households during the same period (from 3.6 to 6.1 percent) (*Condition of Education 1997* 212). Parents in poor households, in other words, are the least able to prepare their children for success in an educational system that defines literacy in terms of being able to operate in technologically based communication environments, many of which are costly and far from universally accessible in this country. Similar inequities are associated with families who live in rural America. For example, rural schools enrolling high populations of low socioeconomic students have less access than urban districts enrolling high populations of such students (*Getting America's Students Ready* 36).

More about Paying Attention to the New Literacy Agenda— Additional Challenges

Given these realities, teachers need to understand as much as possible about the broad cultural link between technology and literacy and how this formation has come to determine not only official definitions of literacy but also the lived experiences of individuals and families.

More specifically, the national project to expand technological literacy is crucial to teachers and scholars at all levels, and we need to address this project directly, systematically, and collectively. It bears on our professional responsibility to understand and work with the complex relationships between humans, the language they use, and the social contexts within which both exist.

Unfortunately, anyone familiar with the traditional values of humanism knows that, as a group, English studies, composition, and language arts teachers prefer that technology remain quiet and well behaved in the background of our lives, where we can use it when we choose—but pay very little attention to it most of the time. Although we are tolerant of those colleagues interested in the "souls of machines," to use Bruno Latour's term, we assign them to a peculiar kind of professional isolation "in their own separate world" of computer workshops and computer classrooms and professional conferences that many of us feel are influenced more by the concerns of "engineers, technicians, and technocrats" than by those of humanists (vi).

It is this same set of historically and professionally determined beliefs that informs many faculty members' actions within our home departments and schools, where we often continue to allocate the responsibility of technology decisions—and often the responsibility of computer-supported classrooms—to a single faculty or staff member who doesn't mind wrestling with computers or the thorny issues that can be associated with their use.

In this way, we manage to have computers available for our own studies, in support of our classes and our profession, but we also relegate these technologies to the background of our professional lives. As a result, computers are rapidly becoming invisible. When we don't have to pay attention to machines, we remain free to focus on the teaching and study of language, the stuff of real intellectual and social concern.

As literacy educators, we prefer things to be arranged this way because computers—when they are too much in our face, as unfamiliar technology generally is—can suggest a kind of cultural strangeness that is off-putting. We are much more used to dealing with older technologies like print, a technology old enough that we don't have to think so much about it, old enough that it doesn't call such immediate attention to the social or material conditions associated with its use. Books are relatively cheap, they are generally accessible to students, districts, families, and educators; and they are acknowledged by our peers to be the appropriate tools to use for teaching and learning. As a result, our recognition of the material conditions associated with books has faded into the background of our imagination. Although we understand on a tacit level that the print technology in which we invest so readily, and in which we ask students to invest, contributes to our own wallets (e.g., when we edit or write textbooks) or to our own status in the profession and in the public eye (in terms of performance assessment, promotion, and sometimes salary rewards), we seldom notice it.

There are other things that don't often occur to us. When we use the more familiar technology of books, for instance, it is mostly within a familiar ideological system that allows us to ignore, except for some occasional twinges of conscience, the persistence of print and our role in this persistence. It allows us to ignore the understanding that print literacy functions as a cultural system, as Lester Faigley and others (Gee; Graff; Stuckey; Rose) have noted, that not only carries and distributes enlightened ideas but also supports a pattern of continuing illiteracy in this country.

I offer this example to suggest that literacy teachers, educated in the humanist tradition, generally prefer our technologies and the material conditions associated so closely with them to remain in the background for obvious reasons, and the belief systems we construct in connection with various technologies allow us to undertake a comfortable process of naturalization. In the case of computers, we have convinced ourselves that we and the students with whom we work are made of much finer stuff than the machine in our midst, and we are determined to maintain this state of affairs.

This ideological position, however, has other effects and costs. As a result of the negative value we generally assign to discussions about computers, our professional organizations continue to deal with technology in what is essentially a piecemeal fashion. We now think of computers, for instance, as a simple tool that individual teachers can use or ignore in their classrooms as they choose but also one that the profession, as a whole, with just a few notable exceptions, need not address systematically.

Exacerbating this situation is the fact that literacy teachers and scholars generally claim allegiance to one of two camps. Computer-*using* teachers enthusiastically endorse computers in their classrooms, but all too often they do not teach students how to pay critical attention to the issues generated by technology use. Teachers who choose *not* to use computers in class believe that their decision absolves them and their students from paying critical attention to technology issues. And so, as a profession, we have given technology issues precious little focused attention over the years.

We have begun to recognize that allowing ourselves the luxury of such positions is not only misguided but also dangerously short-sighted. We are teaching students who *must* know how to communicate in an increasingly technological world. Further, these students need not only have the capability of using computers. They must also have the ability to understand, from a critical perspective, the social and cultural contexts for on-line discourse and communication and the ways in which electronic communication environments have become essential parts of our cultural understanding of what it means to be literate.

These recognitions are only the barest of starting points. They have brought literacy educators only to the point of *using* computers—or not doing so—but not to the more important point of *thinking* about what we are doing and trying to understand the implications of our actions. It has become increasingly clear over the past five years that we also have two much larger and more complicated obligations: first, we must try to understand—to *pay attention to*—how technology is now inextricably linked to literacy and literacy education in this country; and, second, we must help colleagues, students, administrators, politicians, and other Americans gain some increasingly critical and productive perspective on technological literacy.

2 / The Problem of Polemic: Representations of Technological Literacy in the Popular Press

I sit at my keyboard and . . . spew out my words easily, unthinkingly, at no psychic cost to myself, and launch them into a world already drowning in its own babble. The swelling torrent threatens to engulf every deeply considered word. . . . [T]here is no lucent depth of meaning, no set purpose—but only the random discharge of surface energies. . . .

The word's dreary passage through the information machine may enable us to recognize the desiccation of meaning, the mechanization of thinking to which we ourselves are liable. (Talbot 182–93)

Technological Literacy: A Step Forward or a Step Back?

One of the most visible forums in which Americans discuss their views of technology and its relationship with literacy is the popular press. Popular news magazines such as *Time, Newsweek,* and *Scientific American* have run regular thematic issues on computers and their use as literacy tools for the past decade. And publishers have found a market in trade books that address technology and literacy issues: Marshall McLuhan's *Gutenberg Galaxy* (1962), Michael Schrage's *Shared Minds* (1990), Howard Rheingold's *Virtual Community* (1993), Sven Birkerts's *The Gutenberg Elegies: The Fate of Reading in an Electronic Age* (1994), and Sherry Turkle's *Life on the Screen* (1995). These publications illustrate how Americans understand technology and its general social relationship to literacy at this particular time. They also reveal the general values we attach to the national project of technological literacy.

25

Two popular representations of technology currently contend for our national attention in explaining the increasingly strong links between computer technology and literacy that characterize our culture in late-twentieth-century America: technology as a boon and technology as a burden. In the first representation, constructed by works such as McLuhan's *Gutenberg Galaxy* (1962), Negroponte's *being digital* (1995), Rheingold's *Virtual Community* (1994), and Hiltz and Turoff's *Networked Nation* (1993), computer-based communication environments are portrayed as progressive arenas for social exchange and involvement. In the second representation, described in works such as Stoll's *Silicon Snake Oil: Second Thoughts on the Information Highway* (1995); Sanders's *A Is for Ox: The Collapse of Literacy and the Rise of Violence in an Electronic Age* (1995), and Birkerts's *Gutenberg Elegies* (1994), computer-based environments for the practice of literacy are described as contributing to the decline of both reading and writing skills, as well as to individuals' inability to concentrate over sustained periods, the rise of violence, and the progressive social alienation of generations born after 1970. In these representations, both our fears and our hopes for technology are played out dramatically, if not always accurately, in terms of an oppositional relationship. The polemic constituted by these opposing visions, unfortunately, serves to distract us from more challenging social tasks: understanding the robust and far-reaching cultural relationships that support the technology-literacy link and recognizing the ways in which this link serves to exacerbate patterns of illiteracy based on race and poverty.

Computers as Literacy Boon

The first and more powerful representation links computers and technological literacy to the ongoing project of science and to our related, historically determined cultural beliefs in progress, economic prosperity, capitalism, education, and democracy. Given the accumulated tendential force associated with these cultural formations, the narrative of computers as a progressive literacy tool has

assumed a particular potency for Americans. Further, with its uto-
pian underpinnings, this narrative expresses most directly American *hopes* for technology, rather than the *realities* characterizing
technology's link to literacy in official instructional contexts.

Quite simply put, this representation tells us that computers in
the hands of right-minded Americans working within a fair and
democratic system can help us make the world a better place in
which to live—a global (and networked) village—especially when
technology is refined in its design by scientists and engineers, who
are committed to making it serve the needs of human beings, and
when it is carefully legislated by a democratic federal government
committed to looking after the best interests of citizens. According
to this representation, American technological know-how, fostered
within our system of education, has helped us develop the knowledge and skills needed to create a national information infrastructure that will link people around the country in productive ways;
support ongoing and much needed research on health, scientific
puzzles, and national defense projects; and contribute to the vital
and democratic involvement of all citizens in decisions of national
importance.

The fact that technology is linked with the social formations of
science, economic prosperity, education, capitalism, and democracy
lends this entire story a potent cumulative power. Computers, according to this narrative, are the latest in a long line of technological discoveries that will continue to make the world a better place
by extending the reach and the control of humankind, most specifically the reach of Americans and our particular system of free-
market capitalism and democracy. Designed within such a system,
computers will help us unravel the mystery of human genes and
thus help us find the cure for diseases that have plagued humankind for centuries; they will help us travel to far-off planets and
map the floor of the oceans and thus ensure an improved understanding of the natural world; computers will help us unravel the
mysteries of natural events like hurricanes, tornadoes, earthquakes,
and volcanoes and thus predict and avoid the danger posed by such

phenomena; computers will help us make education more effective and efficient and will help us prepare citizens who are capable of increased democratic involvement.

Two books that describe the computer revolution to the American public, Negroponte's *being digital* and Rheingold's *Virtual Community*, illustrate this cultural representation. Negroponte portrays a digital revolution that is all but accomplished, all but complete:

> Did you ever know the childhood conundrum of working for a penny a day for a month, but doubling your salary each day? If you started this wonderful pay scheme on New Year's Day, you would be earning more than $10 million per day on the last day of January. . . . When an effect is exponential, those last three days mean a lot. We are approaching those last three days in the spread of computing and digital telecommunications.
>
> In the same exponential fashion, computers are moving into our daily lives: 35 percent of American families and 50 percent of American teenagers have a personal computer at home; 30 million people are estimated to be on the Internet; 65 percent of new computers sold worldwide in 1994 were for the home; and 90 percent of those sold this year are expected to have modems or CD-ROM drives. These numbers do not even include the fifty microprocessors . . . in your toaster, thermostat, answering machine, CD player, and greeting cards.
>
> And the rate at which these numbers are growing is astonishing. The use of one computer program, a browser for the Internet called Mosaic, grew 11 percent per week between February and December 1993. The population of the Internet is now increasing at 10 percent a month. . . . Computing is not about computers any more. It is about living. (5–6)

The tone of Negroponte's recital suggests the cumulative power of technology's growth and implies that the pace and direction of its expansion within our culture are less of a matter for individuals and groups to shape or control than to observe and revel in. To Negroponte, the continuing efforts of the computer industry, a fortunate child of the marriage of science and capitalism, will supply new products to fuel the desires and the dreams of consumers:

> Early in the next millennium, your right and left cufflinks or earrings may communicate with each other by low-orbiting satellites and have more computer power than your present PC. Your telephone won't ring indiscriminately; it will receive, sort, and perhaps respond to your incoming calls like a well-trained English butler. Mass media will be redefined by systems for transmitting and receiving personalized information and entertainment. Schools will change to become more like museums and playgrounds for children to assemble ideas and socialize with other children all over the world. The digital planet will look and feel like the head of a pin. (6)

Certainly, Negroponte makes no suggestion about limiting the growth of technology, even on a worldwide scale. Indeed, he describes how computer technology—informed by American science, fueled by the engine of multinational capitalism—will help form a global network that will transform the values of our nation and others into a harmonic whole, erase meaningless geopolitical borders, and create a global village in which all members are cooperating partners:

> Today, when 20 percent of the world consumes 80 percent of its resources, when a quarter of us have an acceptable standard of living and three-quarters don't, how can this divide possibly come together? While the politicians struggle with the baggage of history, a new generation is emerging from the digital landscape free of many of the old prejudices. These kids are released from the limitation of geographic proximity as the sole basis of friendship, col-

laboration, play, and the neighborhood. Digital technology can be a natural force drawing people into greater world harmony. (230)

For Negroponte, the harmonizing effects of computer technology also extend to education and literacy efforts—contributing to increasingly rich and interdisciplinary learning in all subjects, enhanced performance in the areas of both mathematics and literacy studies, and opportunities for exciting, nonserial learning and problem solving in educational environments.

A similar world of connected individuals and groups is sketched by Howard Rheingold in *The Virtual Community:*

> People in virtual communities use words on screens to exchange pleasantries and argue, engage in intellectual discourse, conduct commerce, exchange knowledge, share emotional support, make plans, brainstorm, gossip, feud, fall in love, find friends and lose them, play games, flirt, create a little high art and a lot of idle talk. People in virtual communities do just about everything that people do in real life, but we leave our bodies behind. You can't kiss anybody and nobody can punch you in the nose, but a lot can happen within those boundaries. To the millions who have been drawn into it, the richness and vitality of computer-linked cultures is attractive, even addictive. (3)

Rheingold, too, identifies the links between computer-supported networks and the ongoing projects of American democracy, economic prosperity, and education. As he points out, "The technology that makes virtual communities possible has the potential to bring enormous leverage to ordinary citizens at relatively little cost—intellectual leverage, social leverage, commercial leverage, and, most important, political leverage." This leverage, Rheingold asserts, comes from the power that a decentralized, networked system of computers places in the hands of "ordinary citizens" (4). Even youngsters "can plug these two vast, powerful, expensively developed technologies [a home PC and the Internet] together for a few hundred dollars and instantly obtain a bully pulpit; the Library of Congress, and a world of potential conspirators" (5).

The significance of this decentralized network, Rheingold maintains, exists in the ways in which it unsettles the status quo and challenges the "political hierarchy's monopoly on powerful communications media," thus providing the potential for a revitalized "citizen-based democracy" and vigorous debate in an enlarged public sphere (14).

American efforts to expand the global information infrastructure, Rheingold notes, have been taken up by other countries who sense the value of being linked within such a system. He points out further that such efforts are tied directly to the economic prosperity of American industries.

> In the United States, the Clinton administration is taking measures to amplify the Net's technical capabilities and availability manyfold via the National Research and Education Network. France, with the world's largest national information utility, Minitel, and Japan, with its stake in future telecommunications industries, have their own visions of the future. Albert Gore's 1991 bill, the High Performance Computing Act, signed into law by President Bush, outlined Gore's vision for "highways of the mind" to be stimulated by federal research-and-development expenditures as a national intellectual resource and carried to the citizens by private enterprise. The Clinton-Gore administration has used the example of the ARPA (Advanced Research Projects Agency) venture of the 1960s and 1970s that produced the Net and the foundations of personal computing as an example of the way they see government and the private sector interacting in regard to future communication technologies.
>
> Corporations are investing hundreds of millions of dollars in the infrastructure for new media they hope will make them billions of dollars. (11–12)

Rheingold, like Negroponte, understands computer technology as a vital new tool for enhanced democratic participation on a global scale. Both authors see computer networks as social and educational environments that support far more exciting kinds of communities, teaching and earning opportunities, and literate exchanges than those to which most citizens now have access.

Computers as Literacy Bane

The second representation of electronic literacy offers an opposing, pessimistic narrative about technology, especially in its relation to literacy. It gains its potency, in part, from the fears and uncertainties that Americans continue to have about the implications of the technology and its use. In this second story, computers become a force of distraction, isolation, and alienation. Cyberspace, in turn, becomes a wasteland of pornography, violence, and illiteracy.

In this cultural narrative, computer games, chat rooms, MOOs, and MUDs, the WWW in general become, like MTV, distractions that have seduced children and adults to forsake the traditional values of hard work and application and to abandon conventional literacy values, as expressed in the venerable forms of the novel and the essay and tested through the intellectual habits of disciplined analysis and critical examination. Beset by electronically generated images and texts, and lacking the guidance and ballast of traditional values that a stable home environment and traditional print literature can impart, people who have grown up in the electronic age have inherited, and helped create, a world rife with other cultural and social problems. Such individuals, this narrative suggests, have become addicted to the negative values of cyberspace; mindlessly attentive to the fast-paced, commercial entertainment provided by the WWW; devoid of family values and modernist assumptions about right and wrong; and ignorant of the Western literary traditions and strategies for print-based thinking that allowed past generations of Americans to thrive.

A closer look at two popular trade books—Barry Sanders's *A Is for Ox* and Sven Birkerts's *Gutenberg Elegies*—can help illustrate the outlines of this particular cultural representation.

In *A Is for Ox*, Sanders foresees an increasingly technological culture that is systematically destroying itself through violence, suffering, alienation, and crime. This is happening in part, Sanders notes, because families are not educating children in the forms of literacy that bear traditional values—books, stories, discussions, oral exchanges—especially during the early years. A major cause of this situation, Sanders maintains, is the rise of electronic media, especially computers. He describes the world he sees as "peopled with young folk who have bypassed reading and writing and who have been forced to fabricate a life without the benefit of that innermost, intimate guide, the self" (xi–xii). This increasingly technological world provides a violent and destructive environment rife with "despair and drop-outs, teen-age suicides, gang killings, broken homes, and homicides" (xii).

When young people are "barred from reading and writing by becoming prisoners of electronic media" (xii–xiii), literacy suffers in direct and dramatic ways that have a broad impact on both the fabric of our culture and the lived experiences of families. As Sanders continues, "Insofar as the computer has helped to erase the inner core of the human being—conspiring, that is, in the obliteration (ob-litera = 'the erasure of letters') of stories and storytelling—it has hastened the destruction of the family" (241).

Underlying Sanders's argument are two powerful rhetorical moves. First, the argument establishes a firm connection between traditional values—the sanctity of life, peace, the family—and the conventional practice of literacy, reading and writing in print contexts, the love of good books and their ability to educate readers and influence right-thinking behavior. People with strong, socially productive values, Sanders suggests, come from families who value literacy. In a second, related, and equally powerful move, Sanders associates the *loss* of traditional values and traditional literacy forms—the loss of books and education through print texts—with the *rise* of technology. The growth of technology has destroyed the productive influences of good books on good families.

This second theme resonates with the long-standing cultural fear of technology run amok, technology that somehow escapes the control of its makers and achieves its own agency. This theme has been repeated often during historical periods in which new technologies have exerted more visible influences on cultures, as evidenced by works such as Mary Shelley's *Frankenstein* and Nathaniel Hawthorne's "The Birthmark." Arguments based on this theme generate power, in part, by aligning themselves with the ongoing human observations of the ways in which technologies exceed or overflow the original intentions of their makers.

To Sanders, "reading and writing" refers to print literacy and not to the literacy practices of reading and writing on computers. In fact, Sanders maintains, literacy and computers are antithetical.

> [C]alling in more computer power will only exacerbate the problem; locking students onto a screen, especially in the name of having them appreciate language's potential for power and play, destroys their literacy by robbing them of the internalized text as a psychosocial frame of reference. In the end the computer moves them closer and closer to illiteracy. . . .
>
> The computer now acts to remove that internalized text [instilled by early oral language exchanges between parents and children] and to replace it with the model of the screen. The switch has created the psychic environment that produces the unfeeling, uncaring youngsters for whom human life has become a cheap commodity. (128–30)

This claim, which paints an unfairly dismal and uniform portrait of younger generations of Americans, is echoed in other popular works as well.

In *The Gutenberg Elegies*, Birkerts also describes this problem:

> Over the past few decades, in the blink of the eye of history, our culture has begun to go through what promises to be a total metamorphosis. The influx of electronic communications and information processing technologies, abetted by the steady improvement of the microprocessor, has rap-

idly brought on a condition of critical mass. . . . The stable hierarchies of the printed page—one of the defining norms of that world—are being superseded by the rush of impulses through freshly minted circuits. (3)

Although Birkerts recognizes some elements that could be said to be the benefits of "electronic postmodernity," his concern is clearly with cataloging the losses attributable to electronic communication:

(a) a fragmented sense of time and a loss of the so-called duration experience, that depth phenomenon we associate with reverie; (b) a reduced attention span and a general impatience with sustained inquiry; (c) a shattered faith in institutions and in the explanatory narratives that formerly gave shape to subjective experience; (d) a divorce from the past, from a vital sense of history as a cumulative or organic process; (e) an estrangement from geographic place and community; and (f) an absence of any strong vision of a personal or collective future. (27)

Technology, Birkerts concludes, speeds up our lives to such a dizzying pace that the concentration we require to read deeply and satisfyingly is impossible. The prospect of a wired world is clearly a major step in the wrong direction and ultimately involves the loss of the soul of both literature and literacy, the activities that humans use make meaning with the written word:

This electronic mesh is already changing absolutely the way we deal with information. In fact, it is changing our whole idea of what information is. Former scales and hierarchies are being renovated. The medium shapes the message. If it can't be rendered digitally, it can't be much good. Software codes are a sorting hopper; they determine what flies through the circuits and what doesn't. . . . We will all (except the poor and the refuseniks) spend more and more of our time in the cybersphere producing, sending,

receiving, and responding, and necessarily less time inter-
acting in a "hands on" way with the old material order.
Similarly, we will establish a wide lateral interaction, dealing via screen with more and more people at the same time
that our face-to-face encounters diminish. It will be harder
and harder . . . to step free of our mediating devices. (215)

These two seemingly dichotomous representations of computers—
their portrayal as boon or bane—are informative in juxtaposition,
not only because of the ways in which they differ but also because
of the ways in which they exert an identical force on the American
imagination.

Is There Common Ground? Masking and Misdirection

At first glance, the two representations tell stories that seem to be
polar opposites: one view, held by Negroponte and Rheingold, is
that computers represent a major boon to our society, our democratic way of life, and the education of literate citizens; the second
view, held by Sanders and Birkerts, is that computer technologies
represent an extreme danger to our culture, the decline of traditional values and skills, a sure diminishment of literacy education.

In some ways, the presence of two diametrically opposed views
is a comforting assurance to individuals who remain unsure about
our relationship to technology. The dichotomous perceptions indicate in a visible way that Americans are not agreed on the subject
of technology, that there is not only room for—but also reason for—
disagreement on this topic, that careful thought is being applied to
the phenomenon of computer-based literacy, that the whole story of
technology use can be revealed through the combination of their
opposing perspectives.

However, the dichotomous representations are problematic in
the simplistic picture they construct of the literacy-technology link.
By describing computer technology as *either* beneficial or detrimen-
tal, *either* good or bad, they limit our understanding. Provided with
such a simple, bi-directional representation, readers of such texts

(and there are many) are encouraged to take a side—for or against technology—rather than to understand the complex ways in which technology has become linked with our conception of literacy and, possibly, to shape the relationship between these two phenomena in increasingly productive ways.

The presentation of such a choice is, at many levels, a false one and, even worse, one that misdirects our energies and attentions. Such representations, especially when they are structured within the reductive confines of a binary opposition, distract us from the more complicated project of identifying the related social dynamics that underlie the technology-literacy link. Even worse, such a representation gives us an excuse for avoiding our responsibility to address the effects of this formation.

Working from a binary understanding of technology, for example, an individual may choose to avoid word processing by typing on a typewriter or choose not to purchase a computer for her school-age children to use at home. This particular choice, however, represents only a partial agenda for social action and one that ignores the ways in which the technology-literacy link is sedimented deeply in so many related aspects of our culture.

Such individuals may choose not to purchase or use a computer (and may feel righteously insistent in this choice), but they are still intimately involved in a web of technological choices, many of which they fail to recognize. Often, for example, citizens who have chosen a visible path of resisting computer technology (not using computers themselves, not purchasing a home computer) feel they are absolved, or removed, from the responsibility of paying attention to technology generally. And worse, they may come to believe decisions about technology should be made by others. Operating from this conceptual ground, people may ignore many other decisions about technology that touch their lives in less immediate and visible ways. For example, they may ignore the decision-making processes for purchasing and using technology in school systems (especially if they do not have children in these schools); they may fail to recognize the expectations of other families who see technology as a key to economic advancement of their children;

they may fail to understand that the federal and state tax systems in which they participate depend on a national information infrastructure of computing; and they may fail to recognize that America's foreign policy is now tied to technology expansion in global markets. Because they have refused one level of computer involvement in their own lives, such individuals may forget that the political systems in which they participate support candidates who make decisions about technology and literacy issues, that the workplaces in which they labor are dependent on technological literacy practices, that the financial investments which support their families are dependent on electronic communication environments.

And in each of these venues—sites in which the technology and literacy link is enacted and shaped—complicated decisions about technology are being made constantly: How best can teachers use technology to educate students to think critically about technology issues in our society? Should disabled workers have access to adaptive technologies—and to training with such technologies—that can assist them in communicating with others? How much of the national information infrastructure should be supported by federal dollars and how much by private investment?

In these contexts, individuals who choose to ignore technology may also abdicate their responsibility for making sound decisions on many technological issues, for influencing policy or practice. Because such individuals are often armed with a reductive understanding of technology issues, limited by either a pro- or antitechnology stance, their ability to serve as effective social agents in connection with such issues is necessarily limited.

The very same masking dynamic operates in an inverse way, however, for those individuals who assume a stand on the opposite pole of the technology binary, those who call themselves technology advocates. These individuals, who remain uncritically enthusiastic about computers, often come to use these machines without paying attention to the social, political, and economic issues associated with such use. Because they accept technology as a natural and unquestioned part of their lives, they also may come to ignore it.

These individuals, too, often believe that technological decision making—in general, and apart from decisions about their own personal use of computers—is being handled by someone else (often those with superior technological skills). These citizens frequently feel most comfortable turning over decisions about technology to programmers, system administrators, computer experts, pro-technology supervisors, or politicians. These individuals may also cling so tightly to the Technology = Progress narrative that they see all pro-technology decisions as positive or productive. In this way, the nuances of technology issues and the complexity of technological decision making become invisible. Those citizens who take a pro-technology stance may also acquire such faith in the related projects of science and technology that they blind themselves to the complex social dynamics that result from the technology-literacy link—the individuals who do not have the financial means to afford technology, the inequities of technological distribution along the related axes of poverty and race, the ways in which technological literacy supports a continuing cycle of illiteracy as well as literacy.

In sum, our cultural tendency to sketch complex technology issues and the technology-literacy link along the lines of a reductive binary—technology as a boon or technology as a bane—encourages a widespread lack of attention to the complexities and nuances of the issues with which we are now faced. Although individuals investing these two oppositional conceptions of technology often adhere to two very different approaches to technology and technological issues, they end up contributing to a common and undesirable end: neither group pays productive attention to technology issues or to the complicated relationships between technology and literacy. And yet it is just this kind of careful paying attention that our culture needs so desperately if we hope to make change, to effect a productive influence on the technology-literacy link and the projects surrounding technological literacy in our lives.

Part Two

An Analysis of Social Investment
in the New Literacy Agenda

3 / The Role of Government

The federal government's role is to provide the momentum to support state and local efforts to meet the Technology Literacy Challenge. This is done through leadership, targeted funding, and support for activities that will catalyze national action. (*Getting America's Students Ready* 6)

At its heart [the Technology Literacy Challenge] are four concrete goals that help define the task at hand:

- All teachers in the nation will have the training and support they need to help students learn using the information superhighway. . . .
- All teachers and students will have modern multimedia computers in their classrooms. . . .
- Every classroom will be connected to the information superhighway. . . .
- Effective software and on-line learning will be an integral part of every school's curriculum. (*Getting America's Students Ready* 5)

In March, the effort [Net Day], led by Sun Microsystems' John Gage and Michael Kaufman of KQED, wired nearly 4,000 California schools for Internet access. Civic duty aside, business has good reason to be concerned about the state of technology in public schools. (Davis)

Understanding the National Project to Expand Technological Literacy

How does a national literacy effort begin? Especially one of such scope? And why does this particular American literacy project focus on technology? If, as I have argued in the early chapters of this book, the prevailing understanding of technological literacy is incomplete and has led to continuing social inequities, we need to accomplish additional work to understand and explain how the current concept of technological literacy has been established. One approach to this task is to examine the recent history of technological initiatives undertaken by the U.S. government. What problems were government officials trying to address when they created the nationwide initiative to expand technological literacy and began the process of funding these initiatives?

This chapter examines the history of several recent and related government initiatives—undertaken by the Clinton administration on behalf of the American people—that led to the national Technology Literacy Challenge. However, these historical explanations must also be examined more fully within a complex set of related political, economic, and technological contexts. Thus, no one date and no one event provides an easy starting place. As a consequence, this chapter takes two organizational approaches. Primarily, it structures information along the lines of a historical narrative that leads up to the current national project to expand technological literacy, initiated in 1996. But it also digresses frequently to focus on the social and cultural contexts that give shape and meaning to that event: providing related explanations of the challenges faced by the Clinton administration in 1993, the development of the country's computing infrastructure, and the growth of the American computing industry, among other topics.

Political Challenges for the Clinton Administration

In 1993, the Clinton administration faced some very practical and basic challenges, both domestically and internationally. The domestic political and economic situation, in particular, begged for new vigor and direction. As the *Economic Report of the President* (1997) described the situation in retrospect:

> For more than two decades America has faced serious
> problems: productivity growth has been slower than in the

past, income inequity has increased, and poverty has persisted. In addition, serious challenges loom for the future, such as the aging of the baby boom, which threatens to create severe fiscal strains in the next century. (18)

Exacerbating these problems was an intimidating budget deficit, high unemployment in certain sectors of the American economy, and continuing inflation (3). Also, the nation's educational system had come under intense scrutiny. A 1989 education summit, sponsored by President George Bush, acknowledged:

> A broad consensus exists among state leaders, business leaders, parents, and the education community regarding the overall direction education reform needs to take. This consensus centers on raising academic standards; measuring student and school performance against those standards; providing schools and educators the tools, skills, and resources needed to prepare students to reach the standards; and holding schools accountable for the results. ("Introduction," *Goals 2000*)

In the areas of foreign affairs, the political and economic landscape was equally challenging. For four decades, America had participated in projects designed to further international economic development and growth through the creation of a stable and predictable international economic environment. Among the projects that received support were the creation of the International Monetary Fund; the initial decolonization of much of Africa, Asia, the Middle East, the Pacific Rim, and the Caribbean; and the support of emerging economies in Asia and Latin America. By 1993, these national efforts, along with the waning of the cold war and the failure of communism had led, at least according to the interpretation of many American analysts, to a series of related effects. Among them, the global expansion of international economies, the increasing industrialization of developing countries of East Asia and Latin America, and the opening of increasingly competitive global markets. All of these factors, while recognized as positive developments globally, were also recognized by American leaders as potentially threatening to the economic and political primacy that the United States had enjoyed immediately following World War II (*Economic Report of the President* 235–57).

The Clinton administration, facing this global context, recognized its duty to safeguard the interests of Americans while encouraging the global changes that Americans viewed as positive, including the spread of democracy, the opening of free-market economies, and the continuing development of underdeveloped countries. Even if all other efforts failed, the Clinton administration's economic policies had to "position the United States to benefit from the global changes" (248).

To ensure success in this regard, the Clinton administration supported a policy of liberalized international trade. This was seen as an essential foundation for the continued growth of postwar global markets, especially markets that could sustain and enhance an increased standard of living for the industrialized world, while supporting the spread of democratic market capitalism. In addition, liberalized trading, which "worked to free the flow of goods and capital from . . . restrictions" (236), had several important advantages.

- It allowed nations to identify their own comparative advantage, "concentrating their production on those goods in which they have the largest cost advantage over others."
- It provided bigger markets that spelled "greater scope" for the gains accruing to specialization.
- It supported the prosperity that Western democracies believed to be the "best insurance against the spread of communism."
- It provided a necessary and natural cultural "corollary" for democratic, free-market capitalism. (236–37)

To take full advantage of the liberalized trading system, however, the Clinton administration needed to define a primary area of specialization in the world marketplace that could be exploited to secure the continued U.S. economic success in the changing global climate described above. In the end, there was little doubt of what that area should be: computer technology, both goods and services. Only technology could have provided such a fortunate occurrence of social and cultural support. Among the many factors working in favor of this obvious choice were such phenomena as the continuing shift from manufacturing to information chronicled by Alvin Toffler in both *Future Shock* (1970) and *The Third Wave* (1980), Americans' general historical fascination with the technological products of Science, Albert Gore's own expertise in matters of technology development, and Americans' fast developing technological infrastructure.

It was perhaps this last factor which provided the Clinton administration with one of the most useful springboards for expanding the nation's technology efforts.

A Short History of the U.S. Information Infrastructure

In understanding the importance of the national computing infrastructure to the eventual success of the Clinton administration's project to expand technology efforts at home and abroad, some readers may find useful a short and selective history of computing infrastructure in the United States.

In 1969, when the U.S. Department of Defense (DOD) foresaw ways in which computer-based communication would contribute to research efforts in the military-industrial complex and to federally funded research projects in universities across the nation, it decided to create one of the first computer networks to handle packet-switching of information among linked computers (Cerf 75; Tannenbaum). Called ARPANET because it was developed for the Advanced Research Projects Agency of the DOD, this network was meant to "link computer scientists at universities and other research institutions to distant computers, thereby permitting efficient access to machines unavailable at the home institutions"

(Sproull and Kiesler 1991b, 116). By 1977, ARPANET connected 111 host computers at universities, research labs, government agencies, and corporate sites (Roberts).

Although the original intent of the network was the sharing of computer time in support of research calculations and the exchange of data, a relatively minor capability of the system—dubbed electronic mail—rapidly became one of ARPANET's most popular features. As Sproull and Kiesler note,

> Computer scientists around the country used ARPANET to exchange ideas spontaneously and casually. Graduate students discussed problems and shared skills with professors and other students without regard to their physical location. Heads of research projects used electronic mail to coordinate activities with project members and to stay in touch with other research teams and funding agencies. (1991b, 118)

Computer networks like ARPANET that served scientists, engineers, and government officials grew in popularity and size. BITNET (Because It's Time Network), for example, was developed in 1981 at the City University of New York, and NSFNET (National Science Foundation Network) was designed in 1984 and put into use shortly thereafter (Hardy; Fuchs).

As a consequence of the increased use of such networks, the demand for network space and capabilities also grew. In 1991, Congress passed a bill authorizing the creation of NREN (National Research and Education Network), a high-speed successor to ARPANET. When NSFNET and ARPANET were connected in the early 1980s, "people began viewing the collection of networks as an internet, and later as the Internet, although there was no official dedication." Once a critical mass of researchers, scientists, engineers, and government officials came to depend on the Internet as an environment that supported their literacy practices as well as the transfer of data, growth was exponential. By 1990, the Internet linked 3,000 networks and 200,000 computers. In 1992, "the millionth host was attached" (Tannenbaum 52).

Each of these projects contributed to the public's perception that computer networks represented effective and efficient literacy environments for the next century, and each project enjoyed significant support and investment from the federal government, in part, because of that growing perception. Networks continued to develop throughout the 1990s as practical literacy environments for scientists, engineers, and government officials and helped to establish the link between literacy and technology.

This link was strengthened further by the parallel development of electronic literacy practices within microcomputing contexts in education settings during the 1980s. After the marketing of the first fully assembled microcomputers in 1979 (Hawisher et al.), for example, increasing numbers of schools began to use computers and local area networks to teach and practice literacy. According to the National Center for Educational Statistics, although only 23.4 percent of fourth graders reported using a computer in school to write stories or papers in 1984, this number grew to 39.6 percent by 1988, 48.6 percent in 1990, 56.9 percent by 1992, and 68.3 percent by 1994 (*Condition of Education 1997* 56).

As the Internet grew, the stage was set for the Clinton administration to plan and implement a project to expand the country's technological efforts, one that would have enormous implications for the role of government in both domestic and international affairs.

Technology as the Economic Engine

Within this set of related historical, political, economic, and technological contexts, the Clinton administration came to identify technology as the economic engine that would help address political and economic challenges. The important link between technological growth and economic growth both domestically and globally had already been noted by Gore and others (see Bell;

Stonier; Toffler 1970, 1980). Such observations, however, suggested a specific economic strategy to address some practical political concerns.

Gore summarized the administration's thinking in 1994 for the members of the International Telecommunications Union in Buenos Aries:

> For us in the United States, the information infrastructure already is to the U.S. economy of the 1990s what transportation infrastructure was to the economy of the mid-20th century.
>
> The integration of computing and information networks into the economy makes U.S. manufacturing companies more productive, more competitive, and more adaptive to changing conditions.

With such comments, it became clear that the Clinton administration understood technological expansion as a linchpin that would serve to reestablish American prominence and expand American possibilities in global marketplaces, while serving to revitalize the flagging domestic economy. This bi-directional benefit of technological expansion is described in the February 1997 *Economic Report of the President*:

> [T]he administration's economic policy has been an aggressive effort to increase exports through the opening of markets abroad. . . . The United States will certainly gain, both as a major exporter of information technology and as an importer, as American industries take advantage of new foreign technologies that will lower their costs and increase their productivity. (27)

Focusing on this primary goal of using technological expansion to fuel both a domestic and an international renaissance for America, the administration identified three practical projects.

- An expansion of the National Information Infrastructure (NII), the networked system of computers that would serve to help revitalize the American computer industry by supporting advanced technological research and the development of new technological products. The NII was also designed to support an increasingly sophisticated computer-based education for students in many of America's largest colleges and universities, and to provide Americans with an object lesson about the immediate social and cultural benefits of a national information infrastructure.
- The development of the Global Information Infrastructure (GII), which would increase the demands for American products on an international basis, while supporting the spread of democratic ideas and free-market capitalism.
- The inauguration of a domestic effort to increase technological literacy—one which would help ensure both an increasingly sophisticated workforce that could engage in the effort of expanded technology production and an increasingly large pool of consumers whose appetite would help revitalize a flagging domestic computer industry.

Expanding the NII and Revitalizing the U.S. Computer Industry

The domestic arena proved an important venue for the Clinton administration's larger project to expand the nation's technology efforts. Without a vital computer industry at home, a technologically savvy workforce who used and appreciated computers, and strong research and development support, the engine of technology might sputter and die.

With these key components in place, however, technological growth would be largely self-fueling. As the administration's reasoning went, growth in the domestic computer industry required the involvement of a population heavily dependent on computer-based environments for its own literacy practices. Given the increasing pace of technological change, such a population would be continual technology consumers. Such a population would also develop an increased appetite for powerful and sophisticated technology produced by the American computing industry. To keep pace with the demand, this industry would need to create more high-paying jobs, which would, in turn, add momentum to the domestic economy. Further, the increased demands of such a technologically savvy population for new products and new capabilities would also pressure that industry to increase the pace of innovation even more dramatically than it already had. This dynamic would result in an expanded exporting and importing capability focused on technology goods and services.

With this project, then, America could revitalize its own domestic economy and expand its global markets for technology and technological expertise, creating a system of domestic and global imports and exports that fed on its own momentum.

A cornerstone of this domestic project was the development of the National Information Infrastructure (NII). On February 22, 1993, the new administration announced the establishment of the NII, touting the project as part of a broadly conceived Technology Initiative (Gibbons). From the beginning, the NII had an ambitious agenda:

> In an era of global markets and global competition, the technologies to create, manipulate, manage, and use information are of strategic importance for the United States. Those technologies will help U.S. businesses remain competitive and create challenging, high-paying jobs. They will also fuel economic growth which, in turn, will generate a steadily increasing standard of living for all Americans . . . the development of a national information infrastructure (NII) that enables all Americans to access information and communicate with each other using voice, data, image, or video at any time, anywhere. By encouraging private sector investment in the NII's development, and through government programs to improve access to essen-

tial services, we will promote U.S. competitiveness, job creation, and solutions to pressing social problems. (*National Information Infrastructure* 5)

The Technology Initiative undertaken to support the NII had the goal of establishing the network as a site within which a technologically savvy citizenry could "create, manipulate, manage, and use information" (5). An early report, *The National Information Infrastructure: Agenda for Action* (1993), also clearly indicated the importance of this site for electronic literacy practices, mentioning specifically its potential for contributing to the United States' continued economic progress, global and domestic competitiveness, and world leadership. And while the cost of the NII was significant—both in terms of dollars and effort—it promised a "steadily increasing standard of living for all Americans," "job creation," and "solutions to pressing social problems" (5). In particular, the report identified the following benefits of the NII:

- as much as $300 billion annually in new sales in various industries (estimated by the Computer Systems Policy Project),
- an increase in the GDP from $194 billion and the GNP by $321 billion by the year 2007, and an increase in productivity by 20 to 40 percent,
- as many as 300,000 jobs in the next 10–15 years. (13)

The national communicative space to be supported by the NII was to be shaped with the help of a number of groups including representatives of business, industry, government, and public organizations. And although these groups differed widely in their membership and goals, they generally shared the Clinton administration's vision of the NII as a democratic public utility that could serve various communication purposes and have a broadly positive economic impact. For example, the Telecommunications Policy Roundtable, a coalition of more than seventy public interest organizations hoping to influence the design of the NII, articulated the following goals:

- Universal access: All people should have affordable access to the
  ... NII. Fundamental to life, liberty, and the pursuit of happi-
  ness in the Information Age is access to video, audio, and data
  networks that provide a broad range of news, public affairs, education, health, and government information and services. . . . Information that is essential in order to fully participate in a democratic society should be provided free.
- Freedom to communicate: The NII should enable all people to
  effectively exercise their fundamental right to communicate.
  Freedom of speech should be protected and fostered by the new
  information infrastructure, guaranteeing the right of every person to communicate easily, affordably, and effectively.
- Vital civic sector: The NII must have a vital civic sector at its
  core . . . which enables the meaningful participation of all segments of our pluralistic society.
- Diverse and competitive marketplace: The NII should ensure
  competition among ideas and information providers.
    The NII must be designed to foster a healthy marketplace of
  ideas, where a full range of viewpoints is expressed and robust
  debate is stimulated.
- Equitable workplace: New technologies should be used to enhance the quality of work and to promote equity in the workplace. . . . Workers should share the benefits of increased productivity that these technologies make possible.
- Privacy: Privacy should be carefully protected and extended.
- Democratic policy making: The public should be fully involved
  in policy making for the NII. ("Renewing the Commitment to a
  Public Interest Telecommunications Policy" 107–8)

Over the next three years, as the NII effort unfolded, the domestic agenda identified by the Clinton administration moved into
high gear. Sales in domestic radio, television, and computer stores,
for instance, which showed a steady increase ($24.3 million in
1990, $25.3 million in 1991, $27.4 million in 1992, $31.7 million
in 1993), then soared to $39.4 million in 1994 and to $45.9 million
in 1995 ("Retail Trade—Sales by Kind of Business"). And while it

would be wrong to attribute overall growth in the American economy to any single economic sector, technology efforts did seem to be paying off. As the economic analysts were able to conclude by February 1997, "policies aimed at increased support for science and technology" were "obviously strong candidates" for the nation's economic revitalization and the acceleration of its productivity (*Economic Report of the President* 30). During this same period, the Gross Domestic Product also rose, from $6.4 trillion in the first quarter of 1993 to $7.4 trillion in the first quarter of 1996 (300).

Developing the GII and Expanding International Markets for American Technology

If America wanted to expand its efforts to control world markets, increase the vigor of its economic base, and continue exerting power as a leader of nations, it had to step up its export of technology: creating new kinds of information technologies as manufactured goods and developing the expertise to design, create, and operate large computer networks and to market these support services to other countries. To lay the groundwork for this effort, Clinton and Gore began to push for a Global Information Infrastructure (GII), a worldwide version of the national information superhighway, which Gore described in a speech to the International Telecommunication Union in Buenos Aries Argentina in March 1994.

The GII had two broad goals that related directly to the Clinton administration's domestic and international economic policies. First, the GII was designed to increase the worldwide markets for American technologies and expertise by encouraging a range of developing countries to establish and become increasingly dependent on network computing environments. These markets, the reasoning went, would be long-lived: as the GII was being developed and as long as it was being used, countries would need American technology, and they would provide technology-based businesses in the United States with a continued market for electronic products. Such a system also set up increased possibilities for long-term reliance on the services provided by technicians trained in the development and use of American-made technology, operating systems, software, and networks.

As Gore (1994) noted, the global project of creating a GII would require a great deal of assistance in terms of technological and infrastructure support from American companies and government agencies that had developed similar systems.

> [W]e can use the Global Information Infrastructure for technical collaboration between industrialized nations and developing countries. All agencies of the U.S. government are potential sources of information and knowledge that can be shared with partners across the globe. . . . [T]he U.S. can help provide the technical know-how needed to deploy and use these new technologies. USAID and U.S. businesses have helped the U.S. Telecommunications Training Institute train more than 3,500 telecommunications professionals from the developing world, many in this room.

The second major goal of the GII was to promote the spread of democracy and liberalized systems of capitalism. The GII was to provide forums for democratic involvement and expanded freedom of speech, illustrate the need for increasing privatization of technology resources, and offer a case study for decreasing government regulation. As Gore noted in 1994:

> The GII will not only be a metaphor for a functioning democracy, it will in fact promote the functioning of democracy by greatly enhancing the participation of citizens in decision making. And it will greatly promote the ability of nations to cooperate with each other. I see a new age of Athenian democracy forged in the fora the GII will create. . . .
>
> To promote; protect, to preserve freedom and democracy, we must make telecommunications development an integral part of every nation's development. Each link we

create strengthens the bonds of liberty and democracy around the world. By opening markets to stimulate the development of the global information infrastructure, we open lines of communication.

By opening lines of communication, we open minds.

The Clinton administration's plans to expand the global markets for American technology bore fruit. Exports of American computers and peripherals, for example, which had been rising relatively slowly (22.9 billion in 1990; 23.9 billion in 1991; 24.9 billion in 1992) leaped to 34.3 billion in 1995 and 37.6 billion in 1996 ("Trends Tables: Computers and Peripherals" [SIC 3571]). Further, reports of technology and networked computer use in other countries indicated pragmatic links between the opening up of global computer or technology-based connections and those social movements which depended on the spread of information within a culture and between cultures, the increase of free-market trade, and the rise of democratic awareness (see Gessen; Watson).

Increasing Technological Literacy at Home

The project of improving the technological education that Americans received was also a crucial component of the Clinton administration's effort to crank up the economic engine of technology and keep it running.

If the Clinton administration was to build a viable NII and GII, and use these networks as the symbolic and pragmatic platforms for invigorating the domestic computer industry—and if such sites were to become a key factor in ensuring the success of the United States as a global power in the next century—then a large proportion of the population had to learn to use, design, and manufacture sophisticated technologies in increasingly effective ways.

The education of the population at such a scale constituted, de facto, a national project of enormous proportions, especially because it had to include efforts in all areas of the curriculum. Americans not only had to be able to design and manufacture technology.

They also had to be able to program, create software products, market technologies, and use electronic networks for communication.

In English and language arts studies, this effort meant teaching students to use electronic environments as their primary environments for communication and literacy practices. This task alone was a formidable one in 1993. Although the proportion of fourth graders who used computers as a literacy tool had increased dramatically from 1984 to 1994 (in grade 4, from 23.4 to 68.3 percent), 26.1 percent of high school juniors reported in 1994 that they had never used a computer and 30.9 percent used computers less than once a week (*Condition of Education 1997* 56). In 1996, Secretary of Education Richard Riley admitted,

> [S]o far, America's schools have been an exception to this information revolution. Computers and information technologies are not part of the way most American students learn. Today's students spend an average of only a few minutes a day using computers for learning. Only 4 percent of schools have a computer for every five students—a ratio sufficient to allow regular use. Only 9 percent of classrooms have access to the Internet. (*Getting America's Students Ready* 9)

Nor was the picture any more rosy outside the public education system. Only a limited segment of the American population in 1995 was capable of making direct use of the NII and the GII, for communication or any other purposes. The Department of Education reported that while 27 percent of white households owned computers, only 11 percent of Hispanic, 9 percent of black, 7 percent of urban poor, and 4 percent of rural poor households enjoyed the same benefit (*Getting America's Students Ready* 36).

It was clear, then, that a project to educate an increasing proportion of the American public to use computers and to depend on them for purposes of communication and information exchange would also necessitate massive expenditures on all levels. As a result, it would also require an accompanying effort to convince the

American public that such a project was worth undertaking. The Clinton administration's job was to rally support. From 1993 to 1996, Clinton used the bully pulpit of the presidency to launch three initiatives designed to accomplish this goal. In January 1996, he used his state of the union address to sketch plans for a national partnership that would connect every public school classroom "to the information superhighway with computers and good software and well-trained teachers." On February 8, 1996, the president signed the Telecommunications Act to do this. And on February 15, 1996, Clinton and Gore announced the Technology Literacy Challenge. This ambitious national literacy project aimed to make all young Americans technologically literate by 2000, by calling on "communities, private companies, state leaders, and individuals—including students and their families—to work together to reach the technology goals" (*Getting America's Students Ready* 27).

To make the case that such an enormous project was worth a national effort, Clinton promised that it would pay off, in terms of improving lives, linking the educational literacy effort directly to the chance of improved opportunity for all Americans:

> We know, purely and simply, that every single child must have access to a computer, must understand it, must have access to good software and good teachers and to the Internet, so that every person will have the opportunity to make the most of his or her own life. (qtd. in *Getting America's Students Ready* 4)

Gore, whose early work on the information superhighway had laid the foundation for the Clinton administration's initiative, also labored to muster support for the project to expand technological literacy and to establish ever more firmly in the American public's mind the direct links between technology and literacy:

> As we prepare to enter the new millennium, we are learning a new language. It will be the lingua franca of the new

era. It is made of ones and zeros and bits and bytes. But as we master it, as we bring the digital revolution into our homes and schools, we will be able to communicate ideas and information with an ease never before thought possible. Let us master and develop this new language together (qtd. in *Getting America's Students Ready* 26).

The administration continued to note that such a national literacy effort would serve the purpose of strengthening the U.S. domestic economy and expanding our international powers. This argument, when combined with the understanding that the national literacy effort would improve career opportunities for most Americans, was to prove important. Achieving such widespread benefits for the American public would require all segments of American society to share the responsibility for funding the national project to expend technological literacy. With this argument, the government fulfilled the role of linking the interests of individuals, the state, the educational system, and the public sector to the project of upgrading electronic literacy. As then Secretary of Education Richard Riley described this combined responsibility:

> The federal government's role is to provide the momentum to support state and local efforts to meet the Technology Literacy Challenge. This is done through leadership, targeted funding, and support for activities that will catalyze national action. Building on current educational technology activities, the president proposed the Technology Literacy Challenge Fund. Making $2 billion available over five years, the fund would spur states, local communities, and other involved parties to step forward, produce matching dollars and in-kind contributions, and cooperate with one another. (*Getting America's Students Ready* 6)

The governmental effort was to operate on state and local levels as well. Local communities and school districts were assigned to develop action plans for technology based on local educational needs. Upon review of these plans, states were to distribute funding according to their priorities, with the flexibility to "promote equity among schools, and use existing educational funds in new ways." Both states and local entities were charged with investing in the "technological infrastructure" that would "connect schools to networks" and with making a "concerted effort to build community support" (6).

Government Sets the Agenda for Education

By 1996, it was clear that neither the GII nor the NII could be expected to flourish without an investment of human resources. Moreover, the related projects of expanding markets for American technology on the international scene and sustaining an increasingly vigorous computer industry on the domestic front depended on America's success in educating a citizenry that was increasingly savvy about technology. The domestic effort, for example, depended not only on skilled technology workers who could manufacture computers but also on those who knew enough about computer technology to design, sell, and support increasingly sophisticated hardware and software systems. The international effort depended on Americans who could sell and support technology in developed and developing nations. The only way to produce such a workforce quickly and efficiently was to involve the U.S. public school system.

But educating Americans who could support this project of technology expansion was an awesome task. In 1990, for instance, the total population of the United States was 248,710,000, and the numbers of public school students had risen to 45,166,000 (*Digest of Education Statistics 1996* 24). Increasing numbers of students came from non-English-speaking backgrounds, lived in poverty, and were supported by single parents (*Condition of Education 1997* 2–12). And while American children seemed to be holding their own in reading skills, their performance in science and mathematics was causing concern. In a 1991 international mathematics assessment, for example, U.S. nine-year-olds scored lower than students in five of the nine other countries in a comparative study. In the related mathematics assessment of thirteen-year-olds, U.S. students scored higher than the students of only one other country (*Digest of Education Statistics 1996* 3). As a result, Congress passed the Improving America's School Act of 1994 (Public Law 103-382).

Recognizing that computers had to become not only the business of the public school system but also the "new basic" of American education, the Clinton administration took two practical steps. First, on February 8, 1996, Clinton signed the Telecommunications Act into law to ensure "affordable access to advanced telecommunications service . . . to schools and libraries at reduced rates" (*Getting America's Students Ready* 40). Seven days later, he announced the Technology Literacy Challenge and outlined its major goals:

- All teachers in the nation will have the training and support they need to helpstudents learn using the information superhighway. . . .
- All teachers and students will have modern multimedia computers in their classrooms. . . .
- Every classroom will be connected to the information superhighway. . . .
- Effective software and on-line learning will be an integral part of every school's curriculum. (*Getting America's Students Ready* 5)

To fund this effort of increasing technological literacy, which the Clinton administration and many Americans hoped would pay off in long-term gains in the health of the domestic economy and an increased share of the expanded global technology market, the president asked Congress to "appropriate over $2 billion over five years for the fund," to be "matched by dollars and in-kind contributions from state, local, and private-sector sources," including the first installment of $250 million in his 1997 budget (*Getting America's Students Ready* 40).

Nor were these efforts the only governmental resources being provided to schools. As Riley noted in his 1996 report:

[I]t is critical that the federal government continue to tar-
get investments to address particular needs in educational
technology. . . . The Department of Commerce's Technology and Information Infrastructure Application Program
(TIIAP) provides grants to develop telecommunications
networks for educational and other services. The Department of Education's Challenge Grants for Technology in
Education award grants to school districts in partnership
with businesses, museums, universities, and other institutions. . . . To address the special needs of remote schools,
the Department of Agriculture supports telecommunications links to provide students with access to advanced
courses and other distance learning opportunities, and the
Department of Education's Star Schools program provides
seed funding for distance learning providers. . . . NASA de-
velops model curricula using state-of-the-art technologies.
. . . The 140 schools run by the Department of Defense on
military bases around the world are becoming a powerful
model and effective testing site for the use of advanced
technologies for learning . . . [and] in 1995, schools invested about $450 million under Title I (formerly Chapter
1) . . . in educational technology. (43)

By 1996, then, policymakers in the federal government had
committed fully to expanding America's technological involvement
and thus to a national project designed to increase the population's
technological literacy. Technological expansion was understood as
an engine that would fuel America's international growth and sustain her position as a leader of nations while increasing the vigor of
the domestic computer industry and markets at home. The Clinton
administration had put into place the national and global information infrastructures needed to support increased technological activity and had set the nation's educational sights on a new and technologically rich version of literacy. The time was right for educators
to undertake a new literacy agenda, for business to support and
benefit from it, and for parents to contribute to this agenda.

4 / The Role of Education

The American people . . . have embraced technological literacy as the "new basic" for today's world, along with reading, writing, and arithmetic. Technological literacy is not
just knowing how to use technology for word processing,
spreadsheets, and Internet access. Fundamentally, it is using the powerful learning opportunities afforded by the
technology to increase learning in academic subjects. . . .
Recognizing the importance of technological literacy, 80
percent of Americans feel teaching computer skills is "absolutely essential." More than three-quarters have encouraged a child to use a computer, and 86 percent believe that
a computer is the most beneficial and effective product
they could buy to expand their children's opportunities.
(*Getting America's Students Ready* 10)

Public Education Struggles to Support Technological Literacy

The history of educators' involvement with the emergence of technological literacy shows a complicated parallel development. Educators are aware of the inequitable distribution of technology and
the problems of access associated with a society—and an educational system—increasingly dependent on computers. On the other
hand, they have increasingly adopted and supported one official
version of technological literacy, often ignoring a range of other literacy practices and values in this country and, thus, contributing to
an impoverished agenda of literacy education.

If the federal government's role in developing technological
literacy during the 1990s was to provide the official impetus and
leadership for the national effort, the role of the educational system was to act as the official venue of instruction. Several barri-

ers, however, presented themselves to educators especially in the mid-1990s. In part, these barriers were historical in nature and, in part, they resulted from educators' changing perceptions of technology's benefits. Specifically, those teachers who had once been enthusiastic about using computers as teaching tools grew more realistic.

A brief historical examination can provide perspective on some of the issues associated with this trend. The first fully assembled microcomputers started entering American classrooms in 1980, and enthusiasm ran high. Teachers hoped that computers could somehow help democratize American classrooms. As the culturally informed reasoning went, if the nation could put enough computers into enough schools, then all students—regardless of socioeconomic status, race, or gender—would have access to technology and thus to success through the technologically supported power structures of the American culture. The impetus for the movement to integrate computers into the schools was prompted by at least two important cultural realizations: first, that our society would be increasingly dependent on technology, and, second, that we were not providing equitable educational opportunities to all students within the existing system.

When computers were introduced into schools during the 1980s, however, the expected changes were only partial, and the resulting reforms were no more than minimal. In fact, by the latter half of the decade, educators (Cole and Griffin; Sheingold, Martin, and Endreweit) were noting alarming trends in connection with race and poverty. Mary Louise Gomez summarizes the findings of a 1987 report authored by Cole and Griffin:

- More computers are being placed in the hands of middle- and upper-class children than poor children;
- When computers are placed in the schools of poor children, they are used for rote drill and practice instead of the "cognitive enrichment" that they provide for middle- and upper-class students. (321)

By 1989, computers were indeed present in many schools, but they were being used in ways that sustained rather than changed the inequitable educational trends.

Although teachers perceived a range of benefits to computer-assisted instruction, poor and nonwhite students who most needed the benefits of enhanced educational opportunities, of improved literacy programs, were not getting them in terms of computer-supported education. In 1991 Gomez observed that literacy programs operated on an unexamined set of assumptions about the education of "poor children, and . . . nonwhite children, as well as these groups' perceived abilities to learn with and about computers, [which] replicates "existing models of teaching and learning with traditional resources." She added that it "perpetuates stereotypic assumptions regarding the superior abilities and greater interests in technology" of whites and "students of higher socioeconomic status. These assumptions guide teachers' expectations of students. In turn, teachers' assumptions about learners' abilities and interests guide the development of activities for students" (322).

A similar pattern was true in terms of a continuing gender bias. In 1989, Elisabeth Gerver noted that in programs depending on computer support, "at all levels of learning about computers—in school, in higher education, in further education, in training, in adult education classes, and in independent learning—women tend to be strikingly underrepresented. The extent of their underrepresentation varies from sector to sector and to some extent from country to country, but the fact of it is so ubiquitous that the evidence tends to become monotonous" (483). And in 1991 Emily Jessup pointed out that the gender gap in educational computing had both a qualitative and a quantitative side.

Gomez agreed with these observations, once again summarizing Cole and Griffin's findings: "Female students have less involvement than male students with computers in schools, irrespective of class and ethnicity" (321).

The challenges associated with the unequal distribution and use of computer technology in schools, especially along the related axes of race and socioeconomic status, were to prove embarrassingly persistent. In 1996, Secretary of Education Richard Riley issued *Getting America's Students Ready for the Twenty-First Century: Meeting the Technology Literacy Challenge*. That report, citing a 1995 General Accounting Office Survey, noted:

> Half of all schools do not have adequate wiring (such as outlets) to handle their technology needs. More than half do not have sufficient telephone lines and 60 percent consider the number of conduits for network cable unsatisfactory. Schools that have all of these infrastructure elements are clearly the exception to the rule. Strikingly, schools in large central cities are even less equipped to meet the demands of technology than other schools; more than 40 percent do not even have enough electrical power to use computers on a regular basis. . . . Classrooms in older buildings, for example, may require expensive renovations to improve electrical systems before computers and networks can be installed, discouraging the community from making a commitment. (34–35)

The report also noted a differential ownership of computers by households according to race and geographical location:

> [H]ousehold possession and use of computers and network services is . . . reflective of the digital divide: it is heavily skewed toward middle and upper-class homes. Low-income citizens and black and Hispanic Americans, urban and rural [poor] are much less likely to own a computer than others . . . white Americans are two to three times as likely to own computers as black or Hispanic citizens and six to seven times as likely to own them [as] the rural poor, whatever their ethnic background. (36)

Similar trends, albeit with some complex new variations, have been reported as late as 1998. In *Science*, for example, Hoffman and Novak (390–91) identified the following findings:

- [O]verall, whites were significantly more likely than African Americans to have a home computer in their household. Whites were also slightly more likely to have access to a PC at work.
- Proportionately, more than twice as many whites as African Americans had used the Web in the past week. As of January 1997, we estimated that 5.2 million (+ 1.2 million) African Americans and 40.8 million whites (+ 2.1 million) have ever used the Web, and that 1.4 million (+ 0.5 million) African Americans and 20.3 million (+ 1.6 million) whites used the Web in the last week.
- [I]ncreasing levels of income corresponded to an increased likelihood of owning a home computer, regardless of race. In contrast, adjusting for income did not eliminate the race differences with respect to computer access at work. . . . Notably . . . , race differences in Web use vanish at household incomes of $40,000 and higher.
- Seventy-three percent of white students owned a home computer; only 32 percent of African American students owned one. This difference persisted when . . . statistically adjusted for students' reported household income.
- [W]hite students were significantly more likely than African American students to have used the Web, especially in the past week.
- [W]hite students lacking a home computer, but not African American students, appear to be accessing the Internet from locations such as the homes of friends and relatives, libraries, and community centers. (390–91)

Challenges to the effective use of computers also existed more specifically in disciplinary areas. Some resistance to the effective integration of computers in classrooms, for example, came from English teachers themselves. Although these teachers were among the earliest enthusiasts about the potential benefits of computer-assisted instruction (see Selfe and Wahlstrom 1983; Southwell; Wresch), they also helped the profession identify some of the most complex challenges associated with the changing definition of literacy.

During the early 1980s, for example, despite the promise of radical change associated with computers, composition teachers continued to use the technology—and to write about their experiences—within highly traditional contexts for conservative educational purposes. These included grading and evaluating papers (Marling; Jobst), providing drills and grammar tutorials (Holdstein; Falk 1985), identifying stylistic problems (Neuwirth, Kaufer, and Geisler; Reid and Findlay), checking spelling (Zimmer; Harris and Cheek), providing practice with sentence combining (McCann), and helping students improve the overall quality of their writing (Duling; King, Birnbaum, and Wageman; Montague).

The influence of current-traditional thinking (Berlin) on computer-based instruction was exacerbated by teacher education programs in the 1980s and early 1990s. Most schools lacked teacher education programs that devoted sufficient time to examining technology from critical perspectives. Few teachers, moreover, had access to any postservice education that helped them think critically about using computers within instructional settings (Selfe, Rodrigues, and Oates).

Without such education, and faced with administrators who demanded a speedy and cost-effective integration of computers into English programs, composition teachers often resorted to the readily available commercial software packages. This software was frequently written by programmers who had very little experience in teaching English. Moreover, as Paul LeBlanc points out, software packages—such as style checkers—often served a highly conservative function themselves in that they reinforced the back-to-basics movement that supported traditional authority structures within educational settings. Thus, English and language arts teachers came to adopt computers during the 1980s and 1990s, but often in ways that resisted meaningful change, using computers to reinforce older, more conventional ways of teaching. In many situations, computers were used as electronic versions of printed grammar handbooks. In essence, computers were seen as a means of reducing student-generated error in composition and literacy classrooms.

By 1985, composition teachers had begun to recognize some of the limitations of their earlier uses of computers and to realize that it took hard work to use technology in innovative ways (Hawisher and Selfe 1989). Change, however, remained relatively slow and continued to be partial at best. Hawisher noted as late as 1988 that teachers had yet to adjust their instructional strategies systematically and productively to these new spaces: "The real challenge of working in this context [a computer-supported writing classroom], then, is to devise a pedagogy that capitalizes on . . . computers . . . yet goes beyond what we have previously contrived" (18).

Composition teachers, influenced by the social-epistemic movement, were learning to use word processing to support increased peer group work in classrooms (Cyganowski; Skubikowski and Elder); to design computer labs that encouraged collaborative work (Selfe and Wahlstrom 1986); to explore connections between reading and writing while learning how to use computers in pedagogically sound ways (Hawisher 1989); and to carry out research that looked at computer technology within broader social contexts (Herrmann). Despite the best intentions of teachers, however, the instructional change that accompanied computer use often remained only "skin deep" and failed to address the fundamental problems of equitable student involvement, educational opportunity, and power differentials based on race, age, gender, and socioeconomic status.

Elizabeth Klem and Charles Moran, observing two teachers and their classes in a computer-supported writing environment, commented on the relationship between tradition and change as it was played out in these classrooms. They identified several ways in which the forces of tradition, represented in part by teachers who were comfortable with the existing system, and the forces of change, represented in part by the disruptive potential inherent in the computer-supported classroom, came into opposition:

> What we had not anticipated was that we'd see in these new classrooms a persistent and deep-rooted conflict between the teachers' own goals and those built in to the new facility.
>
> It is generally thought that computers carry with them

new pedagogies and that teachers will, in some unde-
fined way, go along. Indeed, computers are often hailed as
"The Catalyst for Broad Curricular Change" (Gilbert and
Balestri 1988). Our computer classrooms were designed,
as noted above, to complement and reinforce the Writing
Program's model of good teaching. The room layout, with
its notably absent teacher-place, privileged a workshop
model of a writing class and aimed to cast the teacher as
a fellow writer and editor—albeit the most experienced
writer in the room—rather than as the center-of-the-class
authority. Moreover, the network configuration sought
to foster a class model in which much of the learning
and writing happened as students collaborated on the in-
process drafts. (14–15)

What Klem and Moran saw was a "genuine clash" between the
kind of writing instruction "envisioned by the teacher" and the
kind of writing instruction made possible by computers. This "tug-
of-war" was "on-going" and "quite striking" because the teachers
did not seem to change their teaching styles to take advantage of the
new electronic environments (15).

Challenges in teacher education and professional development
also proved strangely persistent. *Getting America's Students Ready
for the Twenty-First Century* (1996) reported the following problems:

- Only 14 percent of public school teachers had more than eight
  hours of training (in-service or professional development programs) in the area of educational technology in the 1993–94
  school year.
- As many as 50 percent of teachers have little or no experience at
  all with technology in the classroom.
- Much professional development is in the form of one-shot seminars that are insufficient to bring the teaching profession up to
  speed with emerging technologies.
- Currently, only eighteen states require training in technology for

all teachers seeking certification, and only five require technology training for teacher in-service. (28)

What becomes evident even from this brief historical account are the various challenges that the Clinton administration faced in selling technological literacy to the American public, in general, and to educators, in particular. Although there was a shared feeling among many teachers that computers could prove to be valuable allies in educational efforts, there was an increasingly realistic understanding of the work and resources that would have to be dedicated to the effort of making them so, especially in the area of literacy education. In addition, it was clear that technology was having a limited effect in schools: it was differentially and inequitably distributed in ways that reflected race, socioeconomic status, geography, and gender. Teachers, moreover, were not being adequately prepared to use technology.

Further, as Mary Louise Gomez noted in 1991, the more general social tensions building in relation to education itself were bound to increase rather than decrease, thus multiplying the pressures on the system:

> United States classrooms are increasingly filled with children who are poor (Kennedy, Jung, and Orland, 1986), children who have limited English proficiency (Hispanic Policy Development Project, 1989), and children who are not white (National Center for Education Statistics 1987a, 1987b). For example, estimates of the growth of the nonwhite school population includes a rise from 24% in 1976 to 30–40% in the year 2000 (National Center for Education Statistics 1987a, 1987b). . . . Currently, 2.5 million school-age children speak a language other than English or come from homes where English is not spoken (Romero, Mercado, and Vazquez-Faria, 1987). These numbers will increase as the non-English language background (NELB) population is expected to grow to 39.5 million by the year 2000. (Gomez 319)

These changing demographics of ethnicity and race, moreover, could not be separated from the changing demographics of our economy. Gomez noted:

> [D]ata show that one in four children in the U.S. lives in poverty, a breakdown of these figures for race shows much higher rates of poverty for blacks (50%) and for Hispanics (40%). Of the 80 million school-age children in the United States in 1988, nearly 10 million came from homes headed by a single, female parent (Strong 1989). For children living in female-headed households, rates of poverty are high, rising to 47.6%, 68.5%, and 70.5% for whites, blacks, and Hispanics (Kennedy, Jung, and Orland 1986). . . . Of students who were enrolled as sophomores in our public secondary schools in 1980, 12.2% of whites had dropped out of school by the autumn of 1982; while in the same period, 17% of black students, 18% of Hispanic students, and 29.2% of Native American students left school (Wheelock and Dorman 1989). (319)

The Intellectual and Economic Promise of Technological Literacy

Despite the lack of evidence that technology would realistically help address long-standing educational problems, however, the potential for increasingly effective teaching and learning offered by the Technology Literacy Challenge as well as the prospect of federal funding remained alluring. As the 1990s unfolded, teachers, parents, school administrators, and community members came to see technology as a progressive educational tool that was necessary and appropriate for an expanded American role in the competitive global marketplaces of the next century.

It did not hurt, moreover, that funding for technology-rich educational projects seemed easier and easier to secure. By 1996, estimates of funding from federal, state, and community sources, as Richard Riley noted, ranged from $50 billion to $109 billion, averaging either $10 billion a year for five years or almost $11 billion a year for a decade (*Getting America's Students Ready* 6). In his 1996 report, Riley listed more than $4.2 trillion in state-supported educational technology projects.

Educators began to recognize the link between technology and literacy. By 1990, for example, even while identifying some of the challenges associated with technology, the National Council of Teachers of English had already published a Strategic Plan that encompassed nineteen general objectives, including the following:

General Objective 15: The Council influences the development and shapes the uses of technologies affecting literacies.
Strategic Directions:
15.1 Establish the Council as a resource center for the appropriate use of technology in the teaching and learning of literacy.
Action Plan Guidelines
a. Create an electronic network for members (Task Force, 19)
b. Help members keep abreast of developing technologies and their applications through publications and meetings.
c. Seek external funding from companies for innovative uses of technology.
d. Develop liaisons with groups or institutions concerned with technology in education.
e. Refer to working group 18 listed in Appendix B. [Committee Cluster 18—Technology: Instructional Technology Committee, CCCC Committee on Computers in Composition and Communication, CCCC Committee on Technical Communication, Commission on Media, Assembly on Computers in English, Assembly on Media Arts]
15.2 Encourage the appropriate use of computers and other technologies in school programs for the teaching and learning of literacy.

Action Plan Guidelines
  a. Encourage use of computers and other technologies to foster collaborative learning.
  b. Enlist the aid of affiliates [local organizational units] to identify model programs for the uses of technologies affecting literacy.
  c. Investigate programs that establish cooperative relationships between corporations and school districts, colleges, and universities.

At least one additional factor influenced this educational context. In 1994, the Clinton administration, responding to the public's increasing dissatisfaction with the existing educational system, passed the Goals 2000: Educate America Act (HR 1804). Its goal was to "raise expectations for students by setting challenging academic standards." To accomplish this, states were asked to develop "comprehensive strategies for helping all students reach those standards." Among the strategies suggested were the revision and upgrading of both curricula and assessment, the improvement of teaching and "strengthening" of instructional accountability, and the expansion of technology efforts in educational settings (*Goals 2000*).

Within the Goals 2000 Act, Section 231 described the goal of "Leadership in Educational Technology":

It is the purpose of this part to promote achievement of the National Education Goals and—
  (1) to provide leadership at the Federal level, through the Department of Education, by developing a national vision and strategy—
    (A) to infuse technology and technology planning into all educational programs and training functions carried out within school systems at the State and local level;
    (B) to coordinate educational technology activities among the related Federal and State departments

or agencies, industry leaders, and interested educational and parental organizations;

(C) to establish working guidelines to ensure maximum interoperability nationwide and ease of access for the emerging technologies so that no school system will be excluded from the technological revolution; and

(D) to ensure that Federal technology-related policies and programs facilitate the use of technology in education;

(2) to promote awareness of the potential of technology for improving teaching and learning;

(3) to support State and local efforts to increase the effective use of technology for education;

(4) to demonstrate ways in which technology can be used to improve teaching and learning, and to help ensure that all students have an equal opportunity to meet State education standards;

(5) to ensure the availability and dissemination of knowledge (drawn from research and experience) that can form the basis for sound State and local decisions about investment in, and effective uses of, educational technology;

(6) to promote high-quality professional development opportunities for teachers and administrators regarding the integration of technology into instruction and administration;

(7) to promote the effective uses of technology in existing Federal education programs, such as chapter 1 of title I of the Elementary and Secondary Education Act of 1965 and vocational education programs; and

(8) to monitor advancements in technology to encourage the development of effective educational uses of technology.

In response to growing pressure from the federal government to develop and publish standards that would support curricular reform, especially in connection with technology use, national professional organizations and state education departments began identifying and adopting content-area standards documents. By identifying an official academic curriculum in various areas of study, these standards documents also served to formalize the new relationship between technology and literacy, often echoing the official discourse used in Clinton and Gore's speeches, federal legislation, and continuing national and state funding initiatives. This official identification of the link between technology and literacy gained potency with each documented articulation.

The National Council of Teachers of English, for example, published in 1996 the first standards for English language arts in the history of that organization. Within this document, twelve standards were identified. Of these, the eighth standard reads, "Students use a variety of technological and informational resources (e.g., libraries, databases, computer networks, video) to gather and synthesize information and to create and communicate knowledge" (39).

The language in this standard provides a snapshot of the commonsense assumptions that Americans held in 1996. It reveals, for example, the belief that technological literacy would contribute to individuals' eventual success in achieving economic prosperity and hinting at the benefits of expanded global technology networks:

> To take advantage of the resources that technology offers and to become prepared for the demands that will face them in the future, students need to learn how to use an array of technologies, from computers and computer networks to electronic mail, interactive video, and CD-ROMs. Technology opens up new worlds to students, making available a tremendous assortment of information, ideas, and images. It also provides new motivation for writing and allows students to assume greater responsibility for their own learning. . . .
>
> Students should use computers, then, to compose texts and graphics for themselves and others and to publish their own works. This requires skill in keyboarding

and word processing as students draft, revise, and edit their writing, seeking feedback from peers and teachers along the way. Students should use computers individually and collaboratively to develop and publish a variety of works. . . . Also, extended use of computers should be encouraged when connection to a network makes it possible to correspond with others nearby or far away. (39–40)

The Standards for the English Language Arts also warned that the literacy-technology project faced persistent social problems. Among these were differential access to computer technology for students in economically disadvantaged communities and a lack of demonstrated success in using technology in ways that would challenge students "labeled as less proficient" (41).

Pressure from governmental agencies to support technological literacy continued through educational funding initiatives and opportunities. As Riley noted in Getting America's Students Ready,

To receive funds [for the Technology Literacy Challenge], states would have to meet . . . these basic objectives:

- Each state would develop a strategy for enabling every school . . . to meet . . . the four technology goals. . . . Strategies would include benchmarks and timetables . . . set by each state.
- State strategies would include significant private-sector participation and commitments. . . .
- [E]ach state . . . would be required to report publicly at the end of every school year the progress made in achieving its benchmarks. (40)

In such language, the direct ties between government funding and state educational efforts to increase technological literacy became clear. And these ties, in turn, influenced the content-area standards that were being identified by state educational organizations in response to Goals 2000. Michigan, for example, published a core curriculum for public school teachers in 1995, *Michigan Curriculum Framework: Content Standards and Benchmarks*. Its "Vision Statement" described a "literate individual" as one who "communicates skillfully and effectively through printed, visual, auditory, and technological media in the home, school, community, and workplace" (3).

The content standards for such goals included additional language about technology use. For instance, under "Inquiry and Research," the following language is used:

> [Students will] explain and use resources that are most appropriate and readily available for investigating a particular question or topic. Examples include knowledgeable people, field trips, tables of contents, indexes, glossaries, icons/headings, hypertext, storage addresses, CD-ROM/ laser disks, electronic mail, and library catalog databases. (20)

The language explaining this standard once again demonstrated the commonsense connection that had become established, in the American collective consciousness, between technological literacy and economic prosperity in this country:

> An important use of the English language arts is to understand concepts and to create new knowledge. As we continue to improve our ability to collect, analyze, and evaluate information, we will increase our ability to contribute to businesses that employ us and the communities within which we live. . . . Today, we have technologies that can facilitate this process, such as electronic library catalogs, e-mail, and fax machines. Use of technology gives us more time to concentrate on the most important component of research, the thinking skills of inquiry. (6–7)

Through these official documents and others—published at various levels of the educational system, federal, state, and local—

the relationship between technology and literacy became officially inscribed. The notion of literacy as an activity that would increasingly take place within technological contexts and the understanding that technological literacy would serve as a necessary prerequisite to economic prosperity became commonsense assumptions of Americans. It was within such documents, which directly affected English and language arts teachers, that larger programmatic efforts were enacted as part of our nation's official project to expand technological literacy.

Current Educational Efforts

By 1997, the link between technology and literacy had become so firmly established in the American consciousness and the infrastructure of public schooling that it had become almost invisible. In this naturalized form, moreover, it assumed the cultural status of common sense, an official version of literacy that frequently served to eclipse alternative visions. As William Rukeyser, a former official in California's Education Department, noted in an newspaper interview in 1997, "Basically, we're making some very expensive, long-range decisions in the absence of any evidence that shows this is the solution to the problems of the public schools" (Banks and Renwick).

Related concerns were also voiced by Todd Oppenheimer in "The Computer Delusion," published by *Atlantic Monthly* in 1997. He noted that the Technology Literacy Challenge had been shaped directly by findings from a special presidential task force: "thirty-six leaders from industry, education, and several interest groups who have guided the Administration's push to get computers into the schools." The report that this group produced cited a long list of studies that "proved that computers enhance student achievement significantly." Unfortunately, many of these studies were "more anecdotal than conclusive," and some lacked the "necessary scientific controls to make solid conclusions possible" (47).

To pay the bills for the increase in technology literacy, Oppenheimer maintained, schools were forced to abandon programs that had less social caché. In Mansfield, Massachusetts, for instance, school administrators "dropped proposed teaching positions in art, music, and physical education, and then spent $333,000 on computers" (46).

When the technology and literacy link was raised as a subject of discussion, the public discourse surrounding the project indicated just how potent a vision it had become in the American consciousness. Edward Rothstein, for example, reported in the *New York Times* on the results of an educational survey, noting that "teachers last year ranked computer skills and media technology as more important than the study of biology, chemistry, physics, classical literature or European history."

One indication of the increasing power that the technology-literacy formation had assumed can be gleaned by examining the country's financial investment in this project. Models of such expenditures have always been complicated by a number of factors, including the amount and quality of hardware and software expenditures; the amount and quality of professional development expenditures; the duration and timing of funding; the costs and logistics of upgrading existing wiring in schools; and the initial and ongoing costs associated with connectivity (Coley, Crandler, and Engle 57–58).

For these reasons, models of the funding needed to expand technological literacy in the nation's schools have varied widely. In 1994–95, for example, Rand's Critical Technology Institute estimated the cost of *existing* technology in the nation's schools as $3.2 billion, approximately $70 per pupil, and representing more than 1.3 percent of total education expenditures. The Rand model estimated the cost of upgrading the nation's existing schools to a technology-rich status would run from $10 to $20 billion nationwide, and the cost of supporting a student at such a school would cost approximately $300 (based on a range of computers-to-students ratios at exemplar schools from 11:1 to 2:1). The Rand report suggested that 5.3 percent of educational budgets was a "plausible target" for technology expenditures. Staff development costs estimated from the Rand model are about $25 per student, taking into account compensation for the time teachers spend on professional development associated with technology. The McKinsey management group estimated that outfitting all K–12 classrooms with enough computers to provide a 1:5 ratio of machines to students would cost $47 billion over ten years, at $965 per student, and would represent 3.9 percent of the K–12 budget in the year 2000 (Coley, Crandler, and Engle 58–59).

Another way of determining the potency of the technology-literacy linkage at the end of the twentieth century involves the examination of data about computer use in public-school literacy instruction, specifically in language arts classes. Such data reveal a system increasingly dedicated to the teaching of literacy in electronic contexts.

The 1996 National Assessment of Education Progress (NAEP), for instance, indicated that 87 percent of high school juniors used computers at home and at school in 1994 for writing stories and papers (as opposed to the 77 percent of students who used computers to play games), 71 percent used computers to learn, and 61 percent used computers in a library setting (Coley, Crandler, and Engle 27).

For students in eighth grade in 1994, 82 percent used computers to write stories and papers (as opposed to 87 percent of students who used computers to play games), 76 percent used computers to learn, and 58 percent used computers in a library setting.

For fourth-grade students, 68 percent said that they used computers in 1994 to write papers and stories (as opposed to 87 percent who said they used computers to play games) in 1994, 82 percent used computers to learn, and 48 percent used computers in a library setting (Coley, Crandler, and Engle 27).

In the senior class of 1996, 72 percent had used computers for word processing and 44 percent had used computers in their English classes. Seventeen percent of eighth-grade English teachers and 43 percent of fourth-grade language arts teachers reported using computers for instruction in reading (29–30).

Table 1 provides an additional snapshot of student computer use from 1984 to 1994. Computer use for writing stories and papers

Table 1.

Percentage of Students Who Reported Using a Computer, by Grade and Reason for Use: Selected Years

Reason	1984	1988	1990	1992	1994
		Grade 4			
Play games	71.8	79.0	84.5	82.8	87.4
Learn things	67.9	70.4	75.8	82.9	82.0
Write stories or papers	23.4	39.6	48.6	56.9	68.3
		Grade 8			
Play games	84.1	85.3	83.7	84.7	86.8
Learn things	58.2	73.7	70.5	72.8	76.4
Write stories or papers	15.0	58.4	61.3	73.1	82.3
		Grade 11			
Play games	75.7	78.9	79.0	78.4	76.6
Learn things	54.6	65.3	64.5	72.3	70.7
Write stories or papers	18.8	61.2	68.9	84.1	86.9

Source: The Condition of Education 1997, 56.

increased by 44.9 percent for grade 4, by 67.3 percent for grade 8, and by 68.1 percent for grade 11.

At the college level, similar trends were evident. In November 1996, in a Campus Computing Survey completed by 660 institutional respondents, Kenneth Green reported:

> In virtually all sectors of the economy, schools, colleges, homes, and the workplace, computers and information technology have made the transition from the unique to the ubiquitous. Consequently, colleges confront growing

expectations from students across all disciplines that technology will be part of the learning and instructional experience.

By 1996, it was difficult to find a college English studies program that did not use computers to teach a range of courses involving advanced literacy.

Evidence of this trend is easy to identify in a brief historical survey. By 1996, a special issue of the *Writing Center Journal*, "Computers, Computers, Computers" (Harris and Kinkead), and several issues of *College Composition and Communication* (Daiute; Collier; Schwartz and Bridwell; Rodrigues and Rodrigues; Sudol; Rodrigues; Hawisher and Selfe 1991; Selfe and Selfe) had featured articles on computer use, and the journal *Computers and Composition* had been launched.

By 1998, two CCCC chairs' addresses had focused on technology issues (Faigley; C. Selfe) and numerous textbooks and scholarly books had appeared on computer use in English and English-related studies. These included texts focusing on computers and writing across the curriculum (Jones, Bizzaro, and Selfe; Riess, Selfe, and Young), computers and technical communication (Selber), computers and professional writing (Duin and Hanson; Sullivan and Dautermann), computers and literary theory (Landow 1992, 1994), computers and composition studies (Hawisher and LeBlanc), and computers and literacy studies (Selfe and Hilligoss).

Computers had also become an area of scholarly focus at the college level. The Modern Language Association published "Evaluating Computer-Related Work in the Modern Languages" in *Profession '96* to help department-level tenure/promotion committees address issues of support for faculty whose work focused on or used computer technology. Universities formed committees on electronic publishing and tenure, and *Kairos* had published a special 1997 issue entitled "Tenure and Technology: New Values, New Guidelines, New Values." By 1998, both the NCTE and the CCCC had committees working on draft guidelines for English studies teachers and scholars working with technology.

In sum, by the late 1990s, the American public education system—as the official instructional agent for literacy—had come to invest heavily in the national project to expand technological literacy. Educators at all levels were adopting the new, official vision of technological literacy as a practical way of preparing students for success in an increasingly technological twenty-first century. Teachers had integrated computers into their literacy instruction, into their classrooms, into their content standards, and into their professional lives, thus inscribing technological literacy into the public educational system at multiple levels.

5 / The Role of Business and Industry

Labor economists estimate that within fifteen years, 60 percent of new jobs will require skills that only about a fifth of us now possess. To prepare young people for 21st century jobs, we must make sure they are learning how to use the elemental tool of the Information Age—the computer. (Geewax 6E)

It was back-to-school night with a commercial twist. . . .
   Apple has enlisted teachers at 1,000 schools nationwide to plug its products in an attempt to use its dominance in the education market to boost home computer sales. By persuading teachers to conduct what amounts to a sales pitch, Apple is cleverly using to its advantage the influence educators have with parents and students. (Gellene D3)

Private Sector Investment in Technological Literacy

The private sector shared with the U.S. government the goal of convincing American citizens that expanded efforts in technological research, development, and manufacturing would improve the lives and prosperity of individuals and families. This shared agenda contributed to and supported the demand for increasingly sophisticated computer goods and a growing market for American private-sector technology.

   If the role of the federal government was to provide the initial impetus and leadership for the national project to expand technological literacy, and the role of the educational system was to provide a venue in which the official instruction of such literacy could take place, the role of the business community was to provide continuing energy and pressure on the system, in multiple directions, with the goal of fueling the national project.

   To start the engine that would drive America's economic revitalization effort in both the domestic and international arenas, the private sector had two major tasks to accomplish. The first involved maintaining or increasing the pace of domestic technological development by stimulating the appetite of American consumers for a broad range of sophisticated technological products, thus creating high-paying, high-tech employment opportunities for increased numbers of American workers and fueling economic growth. The second task was to influence and support the educational system as it produced technologically literate employees who could help export high-tech goods and services to foreign countries hungry for their own technological expansion.

Growth in the American Computer Industry

On the domestic front, the computer industry contributed to the expansion of technological literacy by maintaining, and in some cases increasing, the pace of technological development. If the domestic economy of the 1980s was shaped by the design, manufacture, and sale of personal computers and local area networks, the economy of the 1990s was marked by an increase in networking technologies. During the first half of the 1990s, changes were fueled by the rapid growth of the Internet. As an article in the August 1996 issue of the *Monthly Labor Review* noted,

> The power of the devices and networks run by microprocessors and software is increasing at a rate never seen before, roughly doubling in performance every 18 months or so. This trend has caused the unprecedented reduction in the cost of microchip based technology, allowing computers to be used more widely and rapidly. (McConnell 4)

This rapid change had effects in two important areas: changes in the technology itself, which in turn whetted the appetites of the public for more change and more sophisticated products, and changes in employment figures in the computer industry.

Rapid changes in computer products in the 1990s were frequently described as "dramatic" by economists who studied industry productivity and economic effects. Gordon Moore, chairman of Intel, described these changes:

> If the auto industry had moved at the same speed as our industry, your car today would cruise comfortably at a million miles an hour and probably get half a million miles per gallon of gasoline. But it would be cheaper to throw your Rolls Royce away than to park it downtown for an evening. (qtd. in Warnke 18)

Two of the major factors characterizing these changes in the computer industry were an increase in the speed of computing and a decrease in the cost of computing:

> In 1975, the mainframe was capable of computing 10 million instructions per second at a cost of $10 million. Today [1996], the leading microprocessors can compute 66 million instructions per second at a cost of only $2,000 to $3,000. That means the cost of computing one million instructions has dropped from $1 million in 1975, to about $45 in 1994. . . . This incredible decrease in cost and increase in computing power can be credited to extraordinary advances in the manufacture of microprocessors which contain more than a thousand more transistors than was possible in 1971.
>
> The brisk increase in computing power is expected to continue for years to come, according to "Moore's law." Gordon Moore, co-inventor of the microprocessor, declared that raw computing power doubles every 18 months. At this pace, all the computing power that exists today in some of the costliest supercomputers may power children's toys in the future. (Warnke 21)

Broader Effects of Growth in the Computer Industry

The rapid changes in technology had several related effects. At one level, they increased the domestic employment opportunities for workers who were technologically educated. In turn, the increasingly visible need for technologically savvy employees, and the increasing numbers of firms who were demanding such employees, influenced schools to make technological literacy, and related technological skills, an increasingly central priority in the curriculum. As James Aley reported in a 1995 *Fortune* article, "Engineers—anyone who carries around a lot of technical knowledge and expertise—can probably choose among multiple job offers these days" (53).

And this need for technologically savvy employees was not limited to the skilled profession of engineering. Indeed, it was manifested on almost every level of the workforce, as Sanford Nax reported in the *Fresno Bee* in 1996:

> Employees in the twenty-first century—blue-collar and white-collar alike—will have to be better educated and more skilled to accommodate the new technologies that will be sweeping through the workplace, according to speakers at an economic summit held Thursday in Selma. "The new economy will be global, fast-paced, information driven and will require knowledgeable workers," said Richard Machado, director of the Sacramento regional office of the California Trade and Commerce Agency. . . . And he said that high schools and community colleges may need to expand or change their curriculums to train future employees.

The rapid pace of change in the computer industry, then, not only heightened the industry's need for technologically educated employees, which, in turn, helped to put pressure on the American educational system to produce such employees. It also had the effect of boosting retail sales and employment in the computer industry as a whole, specifically in the sales of personal computers for home use and in the computer services segment of the industry.

Retail stores that sold radios, televisions, and computers, for example, increased their employment 85 percent between 1984 and 1996 (Warnke 24). Jobs in computer services—a categorization which, for the Bureau of Labor Statistics, includes custom programming, software design, computer-integrated systems design, consulting, custom data processing, and other services—increased 913 percent between 1972 and 1995. Between 1994 and 1995, jobs in computer services increased 12.7 percent, representing "a sharp upward break from the trend of preceding years (Goodman 38, 43).

Increased sales drove this private sector expansion, and these sales were fueled by increasing numbers of Americans who used computers at work and in school and who had been convinced by the federal government that their success as literate citizens depended on the use of computers. Between 1993 and 1994, sales of home education software increased 88.18 percent, and by 1994, sales of personal computer application software totaled more than $73.8 billion (Freeman 50–52). The home computer market represented a major area of expansion. In a special thematic issue of *Monthly Labor Review*, published in August 1996 by the U.S. Department of Labor, industry analyst Laura Freeman wrote,

> American consumers were expected to purchase 9.5 million home computers by the end of 1995, reaching 39 percent of U.S. households. This is a popularity never achieved by the electric typewriter or the video game. Forecasts have even called for 60 percent of U.S. homes to have a PC by the year 2000. It is no wonder that computer companies are taking the home buyer seriously. More than 40 percent of all newly sold PCs have been going into U.S. homes, and industry experts say that the home market has been growing at least twice as fast as the business market. (Freeman 46)

The growth of sales in the *home* PC market led to growth in software design and manufacturing, information retrieval, and on-line service providers. As a result, according to Freeman, employment in the industries related to home PC manufacturing and sales grew an average of 2.7 percent between 1988 and 1994 and almost 10 percent in 1994 alone. Fifty-eight thousand jobs opened up in home PC–related industries in 1995 (46).

The rapid increase in home computer sales indicated just how successful the combined partnership of the federal government, the educational system, and business had become in terms of expanding the environments for technological literacy. All predictions, by 1996, were that the complex social dynamic driving such sales— if all components could function properly—would continue to operate. As long as computer designers and manufacturers actively pursued advances in technology and passed these advances on to consumers, Freeman noted, computers could maintain their "mass market appeal" (55).

The rapid increase of technology sales during this period can illustrate, in addition, how individuals fed the complicated social dynamic at what Foucault might call the level of "capillary" action (39). The official technological literacy effort set in motion by the government and supported by the educational system succeeded in whetting the appetite of American consumers for increasingly sophisticated technology. As a result, during the 1990s, America stepped up not only its domestic manufacturing of computers but its domestic consumption as well, fueling technological expansion. Freeman explained,

> Among the social reasons for the market change in home-based computer systems is the desire of parents to expose children to computing at younger ages. Also parents are buying computers for their college-bound students, who, in turn, are teaching the parents about home computing. In addition, parents who are either self-employed or working for someone else at home after hours or as telecommuters are shopping for home systems. Although 44 percent of first-time PC buyers cite doing job-related work at home as the major reason for buying their new machine, 38.3 percent of first-time buyers want a computer at home for their children's schoolwork. (47)

The consumers of home PCs, encouraged by the government and the educational system, had increased not only their demand for machines but also their sophistication as users, encouraging the computer industry's increasing pace of research, development, and change. As Freeman pointed out, consumers had begun "calling the shots" by demanding new kinds of multipurpose machines that worked equally well as "tools for work at home or for children's use" (50).

The computer industry, which had catered primarily to the needs articulated by the business and corporate sectors, in turn, began to listen more closely to the demands of home consumers and to align both their existing products and future research and development efforts along the lines of these demands. Home computer users wanted machines that could not only support word processing but also pay the bills, start the coffee maker, figure the taxes, provide an environment for multimedia gaming and simulations, and maintain a membership list for the local garden club. The computer industry, in response, began to produce machines with sound and graphics cards, super VGA color monitors, multimedia capabilities, advanced audio and stereo systems, fax and modem connections, multiple CD-ROM drives and removable mass storage devices, and preloaded, updatable software bundles. The purpose, as Freeman pointed out, was to "give users a complete multimedia system . . . ready to go in one-stop shopping" (50).

International Effects of Growth in the American Computer Industry

Business and industry also had the task of creating an economic environment that would fuel the expansion of global markets for American technological goods and services. In this role, too, the computer industry succeeded. While the pace of technology changes in America and other places contributed to a domestic social dynamic that supported the expansion of technological literacy, it also fueled this country's technology expansion abroad. In a special thematic issue of *Monthly Labor Review* published by the U.S. Department of Labor, Sheila McConnell noted that the changing nature of American domestic technology was responsible for "launching an information highway that is leading to the globalization of product and financial markets" (3). By 1996, Francisco Moris noted,

> The spread of technology . . . shaped the worldwide semi-conductor market into four regions with two major tiers. . . . The first tier—composed of the United States and Japan—are about equal in semiconductor share (about 30 percent reach). They exchanged leadership roles in 1982 and 1994. The second tier is composed of the Asia/Pacific countries and Western Europe, which share equally the remaining 40 percent of the market. (9)

American-owned computer-related firms, Moris continued, had begun to employ approximately 50 percent of their workforce in facilities outside the United States. Moreover, these firms were not only competing in the fast-growing markets of developing countries, such as the Pacific Rim and Western Europe. They were also establishing production and research facilities in these countries, further contributing to the expansion of American-based technology efforts on the international scene.

The expansion of America's technology efforts in international arenas, as Vice President Al Gore predicted in his speeches about the GII, had several positive effects. First, it increased the export capabilities of major areas of the computer industry, such as the computer-services segment.

> Although imports of computer services have grown rapidly, exports have increased far more. Trends in trade balances in both cross borders transactions ["sales between a buyer residing in one country and a seller in another country"] and affiliated sales ["when a company of one country

establishes a plant or other work site in another country"]
of computer services have been highly favorable. . . . The
U.S. trade surplus in cross border transactions of computer
services increased by $1.2 billion from 1986 to 1994, and
the nation's surplus in affiliated sales increased by $6.1 bil-
lion from 1987 to 1993. (Goodman 41)

Second, because high-tech industries could pay lower wages to
laborers in developing countries like Southeast Asia and, thus, decrease manufacturing costs, the computer industry also succeeded
in improving both the export and import levels of some technology
products such as semiconductors. Exports in this segment of the
industry, for example, increased from approximately $15 billion in
1992 to $35 billion in 1995, while imports increased from approxi-
mately $15 billion to $40 billion (Moris 12).

The expansion of the global technology effort undertaken by
the Clinton administration affected the computer industry in many
ways. Not only did this expansion contribute to an increase in export markets for American technology goods and services. It also
encouraged the exploitation of low-cost offshore labor from developing countries, which served to lower production costs of American-made goods. Further, it pushed American firms into developing
international markets. Sales to foreign countries are now vital to entire segments of the computer industry's growth. As Jacqueline
Warnke noted, "Foreign operations now account for more than half
of the total revenues of many leading U.S. suppliers, and some report foreign sales amounting to 70 percent of their total business
or more" (25). American semiconductor firms established in Israel,
Ireland, and Asia, for example, had become not only "economically
attractive in terms of overall production costs" (Moris 10) but also
strategically important "as stepping stones into emerging markets,
such as China and Eastern Europe" (13).

Although the effects of the expanded global technology effort
and the "technological diffusion" resulting from this effort (Moris
9) were multiple and complex, their direction and purpose were

clear. As Gore observed, such high-tech efforts "both stimulate and respond to global demand for new information technologies and services" and serve as "engines of development and economic growth" (*Global Information Infrastructure* 3, 4).

The continuation of global technological growth and expansion and its ongoing positive effect on the American economy depended on the functioning of a complex global dynamic of related effects. This global dynamic mirrored on a larger scale the dynamic we have already described on a domestic scale. It was primarily, although not exclusively, fueled by America as a leading consumer and producer of technological goods and services. Like the domestic dynamic, the dynamic of global technological expansion depended on the vigorous engine of the technology industry to produce technological goods, stimulate consumer appetites for electronic goods, and employ individuals educated in schools that value technological literacy. As Gore described the situation,

> Given the fact that the worldwide market for information technology, products, and services is currently valued at $853 billion, and that worldwide investment in telecommunications infrastructure alone is expected to exceed $200 billion by 2004, both developed and developing countries need to find ways to share in this growth and prosperity. Attracting private sector investment is the most effective way for countries to do so—as well as to improve their networks and services, promote technological innovation, and succeed within the competitive global economy. The reasons extend beyond the purely financial. In addition to providing inflows of capital, private investment also stimulates development of new technologies, equipment, services, new sources of information, and managerial skills—all of which help speed infrastructure growth and improvements, increase efficiency in the provision of services, and permit greater responsiveness to consumer needs. (*Global Information Infrastructure* 9)

The global dynamic, like the domestic dynamic, also depended on an increasing appetite for sophisticated goods and services and a rapid pace of technological change. As Gore observed,

> The GII will depend on an ever-expanding range of technology and technological products, including telephones, fax machines, computers, switches, compact discs, video and audio tape, coaxial cable, wire, satellites, optical fiber transmission lines, microwave networks, televisions, scanners, cameras, and printers—as well as advances in computing, information, and networking not yet envisioned. (4)

Moreover, the global dynamic, like the domestic dynamic, also required trained workers, many of them Americans. As Gore pointed out, the GII was not merely a global network of linked computers. It also involved millions of individuals, including American programmers, vendors, manufacturers, and service providers who developed software and connectivity, constructed high-tech facilities, conducted research and development, set up and administered systems, and trained users (4).

Making the Case for Technological Literacy

It was no coincidence that Americans were best prepared to provide the services needed by the growing domestic and international computer markets. By 1996, the United States was well into the national project of producing technologically savvy workers educated in a system that officially linked technology and literacy. Nor was it a coincidence that the services segment of the computer industry grew steadily (Goodman 41).

But while this kind of prosperity provided its own economic momentum to the dynamic fueling the expansion of technology, the global effort, like the domestic effort, also required additional U.S. support. Thus, the government and the private sector shared the common goal of convincing American citizens that technology would improve their lives and ensure economic prosperity. It was not coincidental that the achievement of this goal would, in turn, provide additional demand for more sophisticated technological goods on the part of more citizens and would continue to improve the economic picture. As Gore described this project,

> An equally important task for governments and private sectors is to demonstrate the potential benefits of the GII to citizens. It is only when people see tangible results of applications that they will begin to appreciate how it can be used to improve their lives. This appreciation is the key to stimulating demand for the services and the content of the GII, which in turn will provide the impetus to remove institutional and regulatory barriers to its full utilization. (*Global Information Infrastructure* 21)

In the 1990s, then, the need to convince American citizens that it was necessary to invest in expanded technological literacy became an increasingly critical task for both the government and the private sector. This involved communicating to the educational community the need for more computer-literate graduates. It also necessarily required parental involvement. Parents had to be convinced that technological literacy would prove both necessary and beneficial to the ultimate success of their children.

6 / The Role of Parents

Eric Thurlow of South Portland learned to navigate Windows and operate a CD-ROM drive before he figured out how to tie his shoes. He knew terms like "screen saver" and "CPU box" before he was potty trained. His grandmother, struggling with a QR06000012 new computer, is intimidated. His parents are amazed. . . .

Between one-third and one-half of the nation's 24 million pre-school age children now have some computer experience, said Charles Hohmann, director of the technology projects for High/Scope Education Research Foundation. (Blom 1G)

Q: What can a parent do to get over his or her fear of computers?

SEYMOUR PAPERT: You can sit down with your child and prompt him to show you something—perhaps how to play a game. By learning a game, you're getting close to the kid and gaining insight into ways of learning. The kid can see this happening and feels respected, so it fosters the relationship between you and the kid. (Evenson 3)

Parents and Their Responsibilities as Agents for Technological Literacy

Previous chapters of this work have identified the various and overlapping roles that the government, the American public educational system, and the private sector have played in the national project to expand technological literacy. A sketch of this complex dynamic would remain seriously incomplete, however, without a similar analysis of the roles that parents and families have played in supporting this national project.

Following the cultural narrative of "the good parent, the providing parent," parents have been asked to assume responsibility for providing early training in technological literacy for their children. In general, this training has taken two forms: first, parents have been encouraged to provide home computers to their children as early as possible in their developmental history; second, they have been encouraged to introduce children to an officially informed version of technological literacy.

Indeed, at the close of the twentieth century, it has been within the home and at the level of the individual that the larger effort to expand technological literacy has been enacted at what Foucault calls the capillary level, "where power reaches into the very grain of individuals, touches their bodies and inserts itself into their actions and attitudes, their discourses, learning processes and everyday lives" (39).

This effort became a focus of parental and familial involvement in the American project of expanding technological literacy during the late 1980s and the 1990s. In general, this involvement was represented as a parental duty, and the recognition of this duty was based on a set of dominant cultural beliefs. According to these beliefs, parents assumed a primary responsibility for preparing young children to succeed in school. Moreover, with the linking of technology and literacy in the country's official venues for instruction, it had become clear that a great part of this success was dependent on the child's familiarity with technology and his or her ability to use technology for basic communication needs. Therefore, as the earliest teachers of literacy and the closest observers of children's literacy activities, parents began to shoulder the dual responsibility of introducing their children to proper technological literacy habits and of making sure that these activities conformed to the official standards of technological literacy identified by the school system.

Evidence of these beliefs and their power during the 1990s is available not only in data about the rapid increase of home computer purchases (Freeman) but also in the popular publications about home computer use aimed at parents. By 1997, for example, several home computing magazines had established a niche on supermarket newsstands, among them *HomePC* and *Computing for Kids,* both of which instructed parents about their responsibilities as literacy educators.

The summer 1997 issue of *Computing for Kids,* for example, sketched the parental role in a letter from the editor-in-chief, Ron Kobler. Kobler recognized the job of being a parent as "one heck of a challenge," but he maintained:

> One of the few things everyone does agree on when it comes to raising a child is the importance of education. If you want to ensure the success of your children, you need to educate them. Teach them how to read, how to write, how to add and subtract. And how to use a personal computer. That's right: along with the traditional reading, writing, and 'rithmetic skills, to succeed in tomorrow's world, your child will need to know how to use a PC.
>
> No matter what you personally know about computers, you need to educate your children about digital technology. (i)

Educating Parents as Early Agents for Technological Literacy

Within such magazines, educationally approved methodologies for preparing children for technological literacy were laid out in particular detail for parents. In his article "PC Parenting: Using the Home Computer for Quality Education," for example, Alan Phelps illustrated how parents were to serve as teachers in the home:

> Authors of a recent study focusing on educational home computer use suggest three techniques parents should practice with their children while they use PCs together:
> COACHING: Showing kids how to do things they cannot do on their own but, with time, can be helped to do by themselves.
> Example: "Here's a way you can add a graphic to that book report."

SUPPORTING: Encouraging children to use computers by pointing out the things they do well.
Example: "That's neat the way you added page numbers to this."
ROLE MODELING: Practice mindful use of the computer in daily life.
Example: I think I'll use the Internet to research that new car we're thinking of buying. (5)

Phelps also indicated the proper timing and sequence of such instruction, suggesting that the earlier parents could begin, the better. Relying on expert sources, he notes that such education could begin as early as age two and a half or three "or simply whenever the child seems more engaged by moving the mouse around the table rather than putting it in his or her mouth." By the age of three or four, Phelps maintained, children should be "working with simple programs without trouble" (4).

Typical of such publications were rhetorical references to teachers and other educational authorities, including writers, developmental and educational psychologists, and learning specialists. Parents should turn to these experts, the magazines suggested, as informed guides to appropriate instructional approaches that could be used at home.

The range of advice offered to parents by these magazines is worth examining. At one level, the magazines appealed to parents' sense of ethical responsibility, identifying their duty to serve as substitute teachers. As educational agents charged with effectively introducing technology literacy into the home, parents were urged to learn about the effective presentation and sequencing of such instruction. Typically, in connection with this charge, *Computing for Kids* spoke directly to parents:

> Whether you know a little about computers or a lot, the articles in this issue will help you as you help your child learn about computing. . . .
> Don't let a little lack of knowledge prevent your family

from enjoying and benefiting from a PC. In this section, you'll learn how a computer works and what to consider when buying a system and its many accessories. (Kobler 1)

At another level, such magazines exerted additional social pressure to extend the control of the official educational system into the home. The advice they proffered, for example, identified parents as the policing agent, the substitute teacher responsible for making sure that approved literacy activities were given priority in the home and that unapproved activities were controlled, devalued, and kept to a minimum:

> "You can sit at the computer mindlessly playing games without really thinking about what you are doing," says Levin, a New York City public school teacher for over twenty years. "Or you can be aware of all the thinking that goes into what you're doing."
> Left on their own, kids of the television generation seem to spend most of their time dangerously close to the mindless end of the scale. . . . The only way to keep the mindful/mindless ratio tipped to the favorable side is human interaction, i.e., parents and teachers. Adults should be on hand to help children understand and process their lessons even if a program claims to be for standalone use. (Phelps 5)

At yet another level, these publications identified parents as the economic guarantors of their children's eventual success as citizens. "If your child shows a particular interest in one of these subject areas, or needs assistance in a certain subject at school," suggests a teaser for one article in the summer 1997 issue of *Computing for Kids*, "one of these products might make the perfect gift" (3). Another article in the same issue urged parents to make the right kinds of hardware decisions as early as possible in order to give their children a head start in the workplace. "As many as 90 percent of computers used in businesses are PC-compatible. . . . With that in mind, it would be to your child's advantage to be familiar with PC technology. When your child enters the workforce, he or she will most likely use a PC at least some of the time, if not most of the time" (Sweet 34).

The Roots of Parental Responsibility

Confronted by the influence of various stakeholders invested in technological literacy by the end of the 1990s, parents had come to understand the importance of technological literacy at many levels—from the predictions of government leaders about the newly competitive global marketplace that was dependent on technological systems, from their own experiences in increasingly competitive and technological workplaces, and from the clearly defined direction of a public educational system dedicated to expanding technological literacy.

Parents knew that educating children correctly meant teaching them to read, write, and calculate in digital environments, and parents knew who was responsible for purchasing the necessary equipment. As the September 1997 issue of *HomePC* put the case,

> When you send your children off to school this fall, you'll expect them to learn the basics—reading, writing, and arithmetic. After all, as the New York–based research organization Public Agenda concluded in its 1995 report on education, such skills are "crucial" and "make all other learning possible." . . .
>
> [T]he three R's should become second nature, so that by the time students attend high school they can easily read a newspaper or a novel, write a report or a letter to the editor, and instantly calculate the price of a CD-ROM that's discounted 20 percent. (Jabs 106)

In part, the potency of this formulation of parental responsibility rested in the commonsense understanding that the world was increasingly technological in nature. Parents wanted to believe that their children could succeed if they worked hard and were given the proper educational and technological education. Few parents even marginally able to bear the economic burden of these charges wanted to risk their children's future by ignoring such advice.

Most important, however, a long-standing cultural narrative, the good parent/providing parent, provided the basis for the role parents were to play as the earliest agents of technological literacy education in America. As good providers, parents looked after the welfare of their children by preparing them for success in the future. In this narrative, parents were charged not only with teaching their children the value systems by which individuals should live but also with providing children with a system of loving discipline that would teach them, eventually and habitually, to act themselves within a similar value system. Another key ingredient of this cultural narrative was that parents had to be willing to sacrifice comfort in their own lives so that their children's lives would be better. To this end, parents were charged with providing their children with as many "advantages" as possible: appropriate food, shelter, home life, and effective learning opportunities.

By the end of the twentieth century, such advantages clearly included computer technology. Journalist Cheryl Jackson sketched this version of the good parent/providing parent narrative, quoting TV show host Tony Brown, who directed advice specifically to black parents.

> What's going to give blacks a leg up in economic development? An apology for slavery? . . . Having public school teachers learn Ebonics? . . .
>
> Wrong again. Blacks need to learn to use personal computers and make sure their children have them at home, Brown stresses.
>
> "The world has turned toward technology and the twenty-first century will be a century of wealth creation with the personal computer," Brown said. "The Computer is the Messiah." . . .

"If you have a child and don't have a computer your child has absolutely no chance of success. Zip," he said. "You have to decide whether you're going to pay for a computer or give a lawyer or undertaker money sixteen years from now for their services."

It's a mind-set that needs to change, he said. (Jackson 1)

The cultural narrative of the good parent/providing parent was also clearly and consistently referenced in the commercial advertising of magazines like *HomePC* and *Computing for Kids*. The effectiveness of this advertising was, moreover, effectively enhanced by both the text and the commercial images of the magazines. Even more important in these publications, however, the intensity of the good parent/providing parent narrative was enhanced by a shadow, or ghost, message based on an oppositional binary term: if *good parents* provide their children with the competitive advantage to the right computer equipment and the latest software, those individuals who do *not* make such purchases are constituted as *bad parents*; if *good parents* sacrifice to provide their children with a digital advantage, then those individuals who fail to do so become *bad parents*; if *good parents* have the time to monitor their children's use of computers, then those individuals who cannot afford this time are *bad parents*. Such reductive constructions, of course, serve to mask the very real material and social factors (e.g., socioeconomic status, marital status, race, education) that directly influence parents' ability to provide support for their children.

A typical commercial ad for three software packages from Brainstorm in the September 1997 issue of *HomePC* ("Give Your Child a Head Start for Life") revealed all of these narrative elements and the values that shaped them. Playing on the cultural expectation that good parents provide their children with the chance to succeed in official educational environments, this advertisement focused on the importance of parents' roles as early literacy educators and their responsibilities to serve as home-based instructional agents for the official educational system. It urged parents to acquire a software package that would help their children develop the skills for succeeding in "school and in life." From this rhetorical perspective, the ad also served to mask its own economic stake in this situation, to deflect readers' attention away from recognition that the purchase of this software most directly—and economically—benefited Brainstorm as a commercial entity:

> GIVE YOUR CHILD A HEAD START FOR LIFE
> At Brainstorm, we believe that essential learning skills and attributes like self-esteem and self-confidence contribute to your child's success in school and in life. . . .
> Get a head start on shopping for school supplies and a head start in life with Brainstorm. A $10 check, instantly redeemable for school supplies will be yours with the purchase of each specially marked package of Chess-Mates, Drawing Discoveries, and Mario Teaches Typing 2 game. Buy all three games and you'll get $30! . . . Give your kids a little something extra. (175)

Bad parents, as this ad suggested without having to explicitly say so, are not willing or able to give their children "something extra." Parents who cannot afford a home PC and the software that goes along with it are not giving their children a "head start in life" and are failing them in this regard.

Additional commercial advertisements for software and hardware products elaborated on other themes related to the good parent/providing parent narrative. An advertisement for an educational software package by Avery ("Open Up Your Child's Mind"), for example, suggested that the savvy computer industry was willing to team up with both parents and the educational system as an informed instructional ally.

> Open up your child's mind to a whole new world of creativity.

> Avery Kids lets your child's imagination come out and play. . . . [G]ive kids the power to create fun, interactive printouts they can be proud of. Turn your child's play time and school projects into a new adventure. (109)

As the text of several additional advertisements noted, the right software product produced by the right software company and purchased by right-thinking parents will ensure children's creativity, scientific curiosity, and ability to read.

> Why settle for the moon, when you can give your child nine planets, Orion's Belt, and a pink poodle?
> Show your kids there's more to outer space than zapping brain-sucking aliens. . . . One small step by you will help your kids make a giant leap in learning. ("Why Settle for the Moon?" 115)

> When your child learns to read early, he's not the only one who looks smart.
> All you need to teach your child to read:
>
> - CD-ROM with 12 lessons and 15 songs
> - FREE flash cards
> - FREE parent's activity guides
>
> Learning Ladder brings you the Complete Phonics Kit, a brilliant way to teach your four- to six-year-old the fundamentals of reading and writing for just $29.95. . . . You don't have to be a genius to see that the Complete Phonics Kit isn't just a smart buy, it's foolproof. ("Open Up Your Child's Mind" 109)

In addition to masking the material motivation for Avery's involvement in home education, this advertisement played as well on the overlapping interests of business, the educational system, and families, enhancing the cultural link between literacy and technology.

In return, the link increases the impact of advertisement itself by focusing effectively on parents' fears. Raised in a print generation, many parents in the 1990s knew altogether too little about preparing their children for life in a world that was dependent on electronic communication (Hawisher and Selfe 1993), and many were concerned about displaying an ignorance in connection with technology. The Complete Phonics Kit, resonating with this fear, focused on such concerns and promised an easy and relatively inexpensive technological solution to early literacy education.

This advertisement also recognizes that parents and their children would be judged within two closely related social systems, the educational system and the private sector, both influenced by shared values on competition and success as necessitated by a free market state. This and similar advertisements suggested that parents could compete successfully if they purchased software that instructed children in officially recognized literacy approaches, such as the use of phonics. Such ads indicate that parents would be competitively judged in their effectiveness, both as parents per se and as early literacy educators, by their children's public performance on instructional tasks such as reading readiness. Parents would be successful, in other words, if they were able to direct their children toward those uses of computers officially sanctioned by the educational system (e.g., toward the use of technology for scientific explanation or for the teaching of phonics) and away from computer uses not officially sanctioned by the schools (e.g., playing games with "brain-sucking aliens"). Parents who could not or did not attend to such official literacy activities, the ad implied, failed not only in their role as parents and their role as early literacy educators but also in their role as citizens.

Masking the Economic Implications of Technological Literacy in the Home

In part, this system of popular beliefs about home literacy instruction served to mask the economic implications and effects of technological literacy. Home computer magazines, for example, commonly encouraged parents to spend money on educational products, appealing to them not as unthinking consumers but rather as the careful guardians of their children's technological literacy. As the introduction to one article in the summer 1997 issue of *Computing for Kids* put it:

> There are thousands of software products available for kids. To save you countless hours of research, we've compiled reviews of some of the best products available in a number of categories. (3)

Or as Carolyn Jabs wrote in *HomePC*:

> Here's a roundup of the best educational packages for third- to eighth-graders—they can help students become competent readers, writers, and mathematicians, but not without your participation. The fourth R—responsive parents—is as basic to a good education as the other three. (106)

In addition, magazines focused parents' attention not only on advertisements but also on prominently displayed information about commercial products presented in the guise of news or feature articles about products. In the September 1997 issue of *HomePC*, for example, a short article on notebook computers focused readers' attention on both Apple's e-Mate 300, a $749 notebook computer designed to assist youngsters as they "do research on the Internet, exchange lessons and information electronically with other students and teachers, and communicate with school officials via e-mail," and on NetSchool's StudyPro, a "laptop . . . built for durability" ("Small Computers, Small Hands" 174). At the end of this article, parents are obligingly provided with ordering information, prices, a web site reference, and a toll-free number in connection with the products.

Similarly, the summer 1997 issue of *Computing for Kids* offered parents informed reviews of software packages designed to support their efforts as early literacy educators in the home. These included Kid Phonics 2 ($35), the Great Reading Adventure ($20), Major League Reading ($20), Reading Blaster Jr. ($35), Reading Who? Reading You! ($80), the Amazing Writing Machine 1.1 ($30), Spellevator Plus ($55), or the Ultimate Writing and Creativity Center 1.2 ($32) (143–53). In such review articles, the magazines posed as parental resources and educational allies sharing the mission of making children better students. Such approaches, while playing on parents' deep-seated feelings of responsibility as early literacy agents, also exploited their purchasing power as consumers in increasingly effective ways.

This particular feature of magazines aimed at parent-readers—the presentation of commercial information in the guise of feature stories or announcements of new products—deserves additional attention. The September 1997 issue of *HomePC*, for example, provided product information about a new $1,600 laptop designed for student use but available only to school superintendents:

> NetSchool's StudyPro laptop is built for durability and can communicate with teachers' computers via an infrared beam. . . . It's not available for purchase by families, but is instead sold to school superintendents to distribute directly to their students.
>
> The StudyPro is part of a complete system called the NetSchools Solution—a local area network, complete with file server and classroom-management software (the Academic Information System), as well as a laptop for every child in the participating school. The average price per pupil . . . covers the cost of all the network hardware and software, as well as two on-site consultants to train staff and students in how to make the system meet their goals. ("Small Computers, Small Hands" 174)

In the complexity of its approach, this relatively short item provides a rich case study of how the economic interests of the magazine and those of the product manufacturer (both linked as separate parts of the larger computer industry) intersected effectively with the interests of parents and educators.

The basic marketing approach detailed in the article, of course, was designed by the manufacturer with the purpose of selling as many computers as possible. The schoolwide purchasing plans promised to ensure 100 percent market penetration. The magazine's decision to present information about the product as it does—in the guise of an informational or feature article about a new product, rather than as simply another commercial advertisement—ensures a close alignment with the economic goals of the manufacturer. By posing as an educational resource guide for parents and offering information about products both in the format of traditional commercial advertisements and in the disguised format of neutral feature articles, the magazine enhanced its value for manufacturers as a commercial vehicle for product information.

Further, parents who read this item as *news* about a product, and not as a *commercially* motivated perspective on a product, might be less inclined to recognize the interested and limited view of the product with which they were being presented—one flavored by the shared values, perspectives, and goals of the magazine and the computer manufacturers who advertise within it. If this material is read as a news item, the StudyPro campaign implies possible solutions to several related technology problems obvious to parents who have any contact with public schools: relief for families from the continuing pressures to purchase and update home computers, relief for school districts from continuing pressures for professional development and technical support, and relief for teachers who struggle with classroom-based technology decisions.

Offered such information, parents who felt increasingly responsible for buying technology might well consider such a product appealing. They might also be encouraged to exert their influence on school boards or in parent teacher organizations when computer purchases are imminent.

Finally, given the cumulative dynamics behind these presentations, it is fair to suggest that they effectively distract readers from some less obvious facts: that the producers of the StudyPro system would receive the benefits of 100 percent product penetration in a particular district; that, under such a system, teachers and the school system itself would come to serve as a free marketing force for a commercial product; and that NetSchool, if it succeeded in marketing across grade levels in a district, would receive an additional advantage of a continuing market for their product.

Parents as Stakeholders in the Project to Expand Technological Literacy

In sum, by the end of the 1990s, parents played an important role in the social dynamic underlying the project to expand technological literacy. Primarily, they were serving as agents who, at the earliest stages of children's development, recognized and valued the official literacy standards promulgated in the nation's schools. They reinforced the technology-literacy link at the level of the family's daily lived experiences. The values that helped shape parents' roles in these contexts were based on a set of dominant cultural and ideological beliefs about educational responsibility as it was located in the American family structure.

Parents had other roles, however, in the project to expand technological literacy. They purchased home computers, educational software and hardware, and magazines that featured computer products. They also supported the educational system and the government, and—when they were convinced that technological literacy would benefit their children—they supported decisions about educational policy that were aimed at increasing technological literacy in America's schools.

All of these roles and the underlying dynamics were revealed in the computer industry's trade magazines. Although these publications appeared to serve the interests of families by providing sound educational advice about how parents could help their children succeed in acquiring technological literacy, they also served the closely related and overlapping interests of government, the private sector, and the educational system by foregrounding an official and relatively narrow version of technological literacy. In this way, they strengthened the literacy and technology link; reiterated the importance of this link in terms of social, economic, and educational success; and reproduced cultural problems associated with a one-dimensional definition of literacy.

7 / The Role of Ideology

[W]e're making some very expensive, long-range decisions in the absence of any evidence that shows this is the solution to the problems of the public schools. (William Rukeyser, former California Education Department official, qtd. in Banks and Renwick 1)

Clinton's vision of computerized classrooms arose partly out of the findings of the presidential task force—thirty-six leaders from industry, education, and special interest groups who have guided the administration's push to get computers into the schools. The report of the task force, "Connecting K-12 Schools to the Information Superhighway" (produced by the consulting firm of McKinsey and Co.), begins by citing numerous studies that have apparently proved that computers enhance student achievement significantly. One "meta-analysis" (a study that reviews other studies—in this case 130 of them) reported that computers had improved performance in "a wide range of subjects, including language arts, math, social sciences, and science. Another found improved organization and focus in students' writing. A third cited twice the normal gains in math skills. Several schools boasted improved attendance.

Unfortunately, many of these studies are more anecdotal than conclusive. Some, including a giant, oft-cited meta-analysis of 254 studies, lack the necessary scientific controls to make solid conclusions possible. (Oppenheimer 47)

The Importance of Why

Government, business, education, and family, as a related ensemble, have exerted significant tendential force in support of the nation's project to expand technological literacy. Teachers who hope to address some of the challenges associated with technological literacy need to understand *why* Americans have invested so willingly in this project.

In part, the link between technology and literacy has proved so potent a cultural formation because it draws from a wellspring of modernist belief in science as a progressive force in society, a belief that characterizes Western thinking in general. In addition, when this belief system is articulated with other belief systems that are peculiarly American, the potency of the technology-literacy link is amplified and focused in ways that make it especially powerful and influential.

This chapter focuses on three related sets of beliefs—involving science, technology, democracy, capitalism, and education—that articulate with the technology-literacy link in ways that magnify its power as a cultural construct. The accumulated effects of these related belief systems lend considerable momentum to the national project to expand technological literacy.

Belief System #1: Science + Technology = Progress

The foundational ideological system that supports the current link between technology and literacy in America rests on a historically determined belief in the project of science and the fruits of scientific effort (technology) will yield a better world for the human species (progress).

This belief gained potency in the Western world, according to Kenneth Gergen, with the emergence of modernity near the end of the nineteenth century. Science as a waxing social and cultural influence was linked to the waning of Romanticism and its adherence to "passion, purpose, depth, and personal significance." Science, sketched in simple terms as truth and reason, depended on a belief in the power of systematic observation, rigorous reason, and rationally designed technological tools. Together, these tools exerted increasing cultural influence on the work of scientists in various fields, and the Romantic trust in the unified self, moral values, and the "ultimate significance" of the "human venture" weakened in proportion (27).

Within this social context, James Wiser points out, the project of science had to do primarily with the practical challenge of bringing the natural world under human control, "imposing design upon the formless matter of nature" (63). And when science was applied to practical fields of health, warfare, and manufacturing, it bore the most "impressive fruits" in the engineering of technologies that improved the quality of human lives: "Medicine and sanitation were improving life chances, better weapons improved new conquests, and innovations in technology—electric lamps, sewing machines, motion pictures, radio, motor cars, and then airplanes—promised a utopia on earth." (Gergen 29). Science and technology were applied as well to the effort of increasing literacy and the effectiveness of public education.

During the nineteenth century and most of the twentieth, the ideological connection between science, technology, and social progress gained potency and exerted increasing influence as a cultural narrative. Indeed, as Martin Heidegger has noted, by the mid-twentieth century our understanding of technology as a way of solving social problems had grown so strong that it eclipsed all other ways of responding to the world.

The ideological equation of *science + technology = progress*, while deeply sedimented in the modernist consciousness, does not fully account for the potency of the current link between technology and literacy in America. The magnified power of that formation grows out of its extended articulation with two more equally potent belief systems, *technology + democracy (+ capitalism) = progress* and *technology + education = progress*, which are themselves aligned with a common set of dominant American values.

Belief System #2: Technology + Democracy
(+ Capitalism) = Progress

A second belief system that lends potency to the link between technology and literacy has its roots in the cultural narratives that

Americans associate with democracy. One reason that Americans have come to invest so readily in the project to expand technological literacy has to do with a dominant cultural belief that the expansion of such literacy is somehow connected with our ability as a nation to maintain a productive role as a global leader. This leadership carries with it an important duty: that of ensuring prosperity for American citizens while creating conditions conducive to the spread of democracy and free-market economic trade so that other nations can benefit from the same advantages that our country now does.

The cultural belief system associated with democracy—and the grand narratives that give it shape—deserve unpacking. Certainly a cornerstone of this system is Americans' faith in the superiority of democratic systems and their conviction that the world would be a better place if democracy were to spread around the globe. Within such a global system, all individuals, regardless of race, gender, creed, or sexual orientation, could exercise freedom of speech and religion; make choices about local, state, and national issues; and engage in representative forms of government.

The democratic system that our nation holds up as a goal is based on the related value that Americans place on free-market capitalism. This economic system, the American cultural narrative suggests, provides an open stage for individuals, regardless of their current position in society, to work hard, invest their own capital and labor, reap the rewards, and take the risks that accrue from such activities. The freedoms represented by democracy require an appropriately unregulated economic environment within which to flourish.

This framework of dominant cultural beliefs explains, at least in part, why Americans have come to believe it is their responsibility to install and support democratic systems of government around the world, as well as why they believe that the free markets of capitalism—within which every individual or group shall be able to make its own way on the basis of qualifications, labor, and personal choice—provide one of the necessary bases for functioning democracies to flourish. Indeed, American thinking holds that countries disagreeing with these fundamental assumptions about democracy and capitalism are somehow flawed and in need of instruction, change, or even military discipline.

When the Clinton administration, in 1993, identified the goal of specializing in the design, manufacture, and support of technology goods and services in order to address America's economic and social ills (see chapter 3), its plans for expanding global markets for American technologies and technological services articulated effectively with this dominant system of national beliefs.

Democracy could spread faster and farther than ever, the thinking went, when supported by electronic communication networks. Computer networks could provide effective forums for the free exchange of information, for the exercise of free speech and choice, for civic deliberation, and for instruction about issues of importance (see Gore 1994; Gessen). America could be the ideal source of such a technological tool, many believe, because its progressive system of democracy and capitalism creates an environment within which technological and scientific progress occurs rapidly and without undue barriers posed by overregulation. Within an educational system based on democratic ideals and honed by the competitive demands of capitalism, America can prepare the best minds for designing, supporting, and marketing such technological tools to the world. In this way, the formations of technology and democracy and capitalism become articulated in very potent ways with the concept of progress, thus yielding the ideological equation *technology + democracy (+ capitalism) = progress.*

Understanding this belief system context can also place into ideological relief the American impulse to construct a global information infrastructure (GII) and to expand its international markets for technology. Many Americans see this country as one that can provide the world with the technological tools necessary for establishing and supporting democratic governments and activities. Indeed, many Americans also believe that they are obligated, as citizens of a progressive nation, to provide inhabitants of less fortunate countries with the social, economic, and technological resources they need in order to succeed in the same ways that Americans have done. To accomplish this task, the cultural narrative suggests, America must educate its own citizens about the use of advanced technologies. Thus, the establishment of the GII and the National Information Infrastructure (NII) become national and patriotic responsibilities, projects undertaken in support of the spread of democracy and the creation of free global markets.

Belief System #3: Technology + Education = Progress

The power of the *science + technology = progress* equation and the *technology + democracy (+ capitalism) = progress* equation are connected to a third strong belief system involving public education and its ability to ensure both personal success and economic prosperity. Rendered in equation form as *technology + education = progress*, this third belief system lends additional potency to the national project to expand technological literacy. Americans are so ready to believe in, and invest in, this national literacy project because they also believe that an educational system informed by systematic technological advances will offer increased chances for citizens' personal success and prosperity and enhance the country's progress as a whole.

Associated with this final equation are a number of beliefs that have become "common sense" in the American consciousness, including the belief that public education must introduce students to new communication technologies so that they can gain access to new kinds of information and the increased amounts of information, the belief that students exposed to these new communication technologies will be able to function more effectively in a technological world, the belief that technology will help students learn more efficiently and effectively, and the belief that learning about technology will allow students to take advantage of increased opportunities for economic advancement. These beliefs help establish a strong cultural association between the project of technological literacy and the values associated with the two previous belief systems we have identified, linking to the values of education, democracy, capitalism, and progress.

The strength of this extended set of beliefs is revealed most clearly when examined within the context of the educational project in general. Public education in America is generally envisioned as a progressive system that, systematically informed by scientific principles of teaching and learning, prepares individuals to take their places in a democratic society as productive and literate citizens who have some understanding of democratic government, some exposure to intellectual issues, and some preparation for making a living in a trade or profession within a competitive, free-market economy.

In part, the values inherent in this cultural narrative about education are those that informed the influential Progressive education movement of 1920–40. As James Berlin describes that movement:

> Progressive education was an extension of political progressivism, the optimistic faith in the possibility that all institutions could be reshaped to better serve society, making it healthier, more prosperous, and happier. . . . Progressive education . . . appl[ied] science to the education of young people. . . . It was likewise concerned with the school serving the well-being of society, especially in ensuring the continuance of a democratic state that would make opportunities available to all without compromising excellence. (58–59)

This belief in a citizenry broadly educated to take its place in a democratic system is a potent and persistent vision and one that resonates effectively in the American consciousness, both with the literacy and technology link and with the national project to expand technological literacy sponsored by the Clinton administration in the early 1990s. The many connections among these beliefs are revealed clearly in the official discourses about technology and computer literacy that were a part of that administration. Vice President Al Gore's speeches about the NII and GII projects, for example, noted that computer network technologies were designed to provide individuals with access to increasing amounts of information so that they could make "incredibly accurate and efficient decisions" as literate and responsible citizens (1991, 150). The national investment in this fundamental belief is evidenced by the fact that such sentiments continued to find expression in educators' claims about technology use well into the 1990s (see Dubrovsky, Kiesler, and Sethna; Sproull and Kiesler 1991a; Lanham).

Another important theme adhering to the American narrative about education grows out of its alignment with the belief system of capitalism that underlies our democratic society, as David Livingstone notes:

> Throughout the past 150 years of industrial capitalism, advocates of the extension of public schooling have repeatedly emphasized two basic themes, solidly grounded in technological rationalist and possessive individualist precepts, respectively: the importance of formal schooling in upgrading the labor force and ensuring upward social mobility among the disadvantaged.
>
> The essence of the upgrading theme has been the assumption that continual societal progress requires a more socially competent and technically knowledgeable populace, and that such qualities can best be assured through formal schooling. The mobility theme is founded on the belief that individuals control their own destinies, and that schooling can provide equal opportunities for each individual to develop his or her abilities. (127)

This belief in a citizenry broadly educated to contribute to the economic health of a free-market system of capitalism is also a potent and persistent vision in our culture. It is connected in the American consciousness with the literacy and technology link, in general, and, more specifically, with the national project to expand technological literacy.

Once again, this articulation finds voice in the official discourses surrounding America's push to extend its technological efforts, connecting the economic formation of capitalism to that of democracy, education, and technological progress.

> The Information Infrastructure bill and the rest of this package of legislation will improve the long-term health of the American economy and help ensure that our children have a higher standard of living than our generation had. It will improve American competitiveness and produce millions of jobs by revitalizing our research and technology base. . . .
>
> By funding the development of new computer technology, this bill will improve the competitiveness of American industry, improve the education and training of American workers, and create entirely new industries. (Gore 1992, 27–28)

> Federal policies can make a difference in several key areas of the computer revolution. The U.S. Defense Advanced Research Projects Agency (DARPA), the National Aeronautics and Space Administration, the National Science Foundation, and the Department of Energy have all spent millions of dollars. . . . [W]ithout federal seed money . . . American firms would not now dominate the world market for supercomputers. (Gore 1991, 152)

> This kind of growth . . . will create thousands and tens of thousands of new jobs. But the biggest impact may be in other industrial sectors where those technologies will help American companies compete better and smarter in the global economy. (Gore 1993)

The vision outlined by these comments embraces what Lyotard might identify as a grand narrative of technological progress set in a democratic and capitalist frame. In its complete equational form, the narrative looks like this: *science + technology + democracy*

(+ *capitalism*) + *education* = *progress* + *literate citizenry*. The plot of
this narrative follows along these general lines: The creation of the
NII and the GII, both examples of advanced technology informed
by the insight of science and engineering, will be good for our country and all of its citizens. These technological projects can contribute in major ways to our country's progress as a nation if we can
educate American citizens, through our system of public instruction, to function productively in increasingly sophisticated technological contexts. Building such global technology systems will help
reverse our flagging economy by creating jobs and expanding the
computer industry. The systems themselves will increase our competitiveness, allow us to open new markets for American goods,
and help us spread both Democracy and free-market capitalism
around the world.

It is primarily within the articulated ideological relationships
revealed by this narrative—where a belief in technological progress,
a value on the competitiveness of nations and individuals, and the
recognition of economic security as a national and individual goal
are connected—that the identity of the project to expand technological literacy was constituted in our culture.

The Effects of Articulated Belief Systems

Because the ideological articulations sketched in this chapter touch
on so many beliefs characteristic of dominant American values,
they have functioned to create an atmosphere of *commonsense* ac-
ceptance of the general link between technology and literacy and
the more specific national project to expand technological literacy.
Within this atmosphere, otherwise debatable projects, interpretations of facts, and discussions of future direction seem outlandish.
Who can reasonably argue with the assertion that young people
need to develop the skills to communicate within electronic environments? Who would bother to argue that students in American
schools may need to pay less, not more, attention to technological
literacy? And so at the end of the twentieth century, the link between technology and literacy seems natural, a seamless part of

American life, and the effort to expand the project of technological literacy within our schools seems a foregone conclusion.

But the danger associated with such extensive, articulated ideological systems, as Terry Eagleton points out, is the effective processes of naturalization that they engender. Successful ideological systems "render their beliefs natural and self-evident" by so closely identifying them with the "'common sense' of a society . . . that nobody can imagine how they might ever be different" (58).

> This process, which Pierre Bordieu calls *doxa*, involves ideology in creating as tight a fit as possible between itself and social reality, thereby closing the gap into which the leverage of critique can be inserted. When this happens, social reality is redefined by the ideology to become coextensive with itself, in a way which occludes the truth that the reality in fact generated the ideology. . . . The result, politically speaking, is an apparently vicious circle: the ideology could only become transformed if the reality was such as to allow it to become objectified; but the ideology processes reality in ways which forestall this possibility. The two are thus mutually self-confirming. On this view, a ruling ideology does not so much combat alternative ideas as thrust them beyond the bounds of the thinkable. (58)

In the case of the general link between technology and literacy in our own culture, this process of naturalization results in what seems to be a coherent and seamless complex of national tendencies.

Through their own experiences, through the speeches of politicians and educators, and through media pronouncements about the power of computers, Americans have become convinced that their own personal economic prosperity and the future of this country as a global power lie in expanded involvement in both domestic and international technological markets. These citizens recognize that achievement of these goals requires that public schools be able to provide official instruction in technological literacy within the formal educational system. As a result, citizens exert influence on their local schools to provide more high-tech opportunities for their children, and they are joined in this effort by educators who have already seen technology-rich educational efforts receive increased government funding.

Given an express mandate by, and funding from, the federal government and the pressures exerted by interested parents eager to ensure their children's future economic prosperity, increased numbers of young Americans are educated to use computers as communication and learning environments within the formal educational system, which undertakes an unprecedented national effort to expand technological literacy.

The technologically literate students produced by this system of schooling form the basis for an expanded pool of technologically savvy and competitive employees who can serve the needs of fast-growing computer-related and computer-using industries, many of which are supported by government programs in research and development. Such employees are convinced of the commonsense need to maintain a rapid pace of technological development and are capable of providing the expertise to accomplish this goal. Workers educated in computer-enriched environments and employed in computer-based industries also develop a long-term taste for sophisticated technological goods, both for themselves and their families. Such employees tend to vote for national politicians who support the expansion of both NII and GII-based efforts, school officials who support high-tech education, and state officials who provide incentives to high-tech industries.

Industries that employ technologically savvy employees invest heavily in a regularly updated computer-based infrastructure that they believe will increase productivity in both domestic and international markets. These companies, infused with resources provided by a country invested in their success, continue to grow and prosper and thus to employ technologically knowledgeable employees and provide financial and social support to school systems willing to produce such employees.

In the more specific case of the national project to expand technological literacy, the naturalization accruing from the related belief systems described in this chapter masks some very real material effects from the national consciousness. Critics note, for instance, that our strong cultural belief in the natural connections among technology, science, democracy, education, and progress affects our decisions about a broad range of issues, including large-scale technology expenditures. William Rukeyser, a former official in California's Education Department, commented in 1997 that technological literacy has come to be accepted as a commonsensical cultural goal. He notes that the ideological articulations of this formation and the tendential force that it exerts within educational contexts are extraordinarily powerful: "The nearest thing I can draw a parallel to is a theological discussion. There's so much an element of faith here that demanding evidence is almost a sign of heresy" (Banks and Renwick).

The articulated belief systems outlined in this chapter may also function to mask other effects of the project to expand technological literacy, including the reproduction or exacerbation of inequities based on race and poverty. In May 1997, for example, the Policy Information Center of the Education Testing Service issued *Computers and Classrooms: The Status of Technology in U.S. Schools* (Coley, Crandler, and Engle), a report which indicated that technology has not helped American education address the social problems that plague our society. Instead, technology has served to reproduce them. Thus, "students with the most need get the least access" to computers in America (11).

Coley et al. reported additional findings:

- Ninety-eight percent of all schools own computers. The current student-to-computer ratio of 1:10 represents an all-time low.
- While 85 percent of U.S. schools have multimedia computers, the average ratio of students to computers is 24 to 1, nearly five times the ratio recommended by the U.S. Department of Education. . . . Students attending poor and high-minority schools have less access than students attending other schools.
- Sixty-four percent of U.S. schools have access to the Internet, up from 35 percent in 1994 and 50 percent in 1995. . . . Students attending poor and high-minority schools are less likely to have Internet access than other students. . . .

• Thirty-eight percent of our schools are using local area networks (LANs) for student instruction. . . . Students attending poor and high-minority schools have less access to LANs than students attending other schools. (3)

Other effects may also be masked through the process of naturalization. For instance, while computer access does seem to be increasing in schools, technology continues to be differentially distributed according to both race and socioeconomic status:

[S]chools with large proportions of minority students . . . have the highest ratios [of computers to students]. While schools with less than 25 percent of such students have a student-to-computer ratio of about 10 to 1, students in schools with 90 percent or more of minority students have a ratio of 17.4 to 1.

[H]igh-spending districts [that are able to spend a high percentage of instructional monies (not salaries) on technology] have an average of 9.7 students per computer, compared to 10.2 students per computer for medium-spending districts, and 10.6 students per computer for low-spending districts. (Coley, Crandler, and Engle 11)

The report comments further on the unequal distribution of technology:

While Title I funding is designed to help poor schools, these targeted resources are apparently ineffective in getting schools up to par technologically with other schools. Since much of the technology that currently resides in poor schools is probably due to Title I funds, it is hard to imagine what the technology level in these schools would be like without this federal funding program. (12)

Although articulated belief systems effectively mask many of the material effects of the project to expand technological literacy, especially those incongruent with dominant American values, they also function to distract our attention from additional causes of failure in the public school system. Much of the failure for the current project, for example, has been attributed not only to the uneven distribution of computers according to race and socioeconomic status but also to the poor education and training of teachers themselves. As the ETS report notes:

- Most teachers have not had suitable training to prepare them to use technology in their teaching.
- In a majority of schools, there is no onsite support person officially assigned to coordinate or facilitate the use of technologies.
- To use technologies effectively, teachers need more than just training about how to work the machines and technical support. . . .
- Many [teachers] feel the need for more technical and pedagogical knowledge—not just about how to run the machines, but also about what software to use, how to integrate it into the curriculum, and how to organize classroom activities using technology.
- Many school, district, and/or state assessment systems rely heavily on standardized achievement tests, which can be a barrier to experimentation with new technologies because teachers are not sure whether the results they are seeking will be reflected in student test scores.
- Issues created by technology itself are also factors to be dealt with, including those related to copyright and intellectual property rights, privacy of student records, and control of student access to objectionable material. (Coley, Crandler, and Engle 42–43)

This complexly connected system of beliefs and relationships also serves to mask the role of universities in establishing technological literacy as a privilege available primarily to elite classes of citizens. As Manual Castells points out, the early involvement of research universities in America's domestic and international project to expand technology research, development, and markets can be linked—through the subsequent rise of the information society in America and elsewhere—to a substantial reduction of lower-skilled manufacturing jobs in inner cities where high populations of the poor and people of color congregated during America's manufacturing boom earlier this century:

> Many of the new jobs of the informational economy require higher education and verbal/relational skills that inner-city public schools rarely provide. Besides, new manufacturing and an increasing proportion of service jobs have become suburbanized, decreasing accessibility for inner-city residents. Thus, there is a growing mismatch between the profile of many new jobs and the profile of poor blacks living in the inner city. (Castells 1998, 139)

The system of relational effects accruing to technological expansion also has cascading effects on a global scale. Castells (1996) traces these effects to several sources, including higher education. "The large-scale initiation to CMC [computer-mediated communication] in the United States took place among graduate students and faculty of universities in the early 1990s." The use of computers for communication purposes will become more pervasive, he continues, when "on an international scale during the 1990s, the graduates that will take over companies and institutions in the early twenty-first century will bring with them the message of the new medium into the mainstream of society" (356). However, CMC and other network domains will remain the sphere of "an educated segment of the population of the most advanced countries, numbered in tens of millions, but still counting as an elite on a global scale" (359).

Castells (1998) concludes that the multiplied effects of the differential diffusion of technology, based on economic and political privilege, are associated with the concomitant rise in poverty, criminality, misery, and inequality in poorer countries and regions of the world, including Africa and the inner cities of America.

The Power of Belief

In sum, Americans have come to invest in the project for technological literacy because the goals and values associated with this project align themselves so well with the other dominant goals and values that many citizens already use as the basis of their worldview. Certainly, the national project to expand technological literacy grows out of—and draws strength from—American's powerful and overlapping belief in science, technology, education, democracy, capitalism, and progress as well as the values that citizens place on the social and cultural formations that grow out of such belief systems.

This potent social and ideological configuration also exerts powerful masking effects. Americans who construct their worlds around the cultural narratives identified in this chapter may find it difficult to recognize the more problematic effects of the Technology Literacy Challenge, especially when these effects are inconsistent with the values upon which this national literacy project is based. Indeed, the power of the articulated belief system that serves as the foundation for the effort can be gauged by the level of resistance in the American consciousness to recognizing evidence of this project's very mixed success. The power of this tendency can also be judged by the ways in which the project's effects, including the inequitable distribution of both technology and official literacy opportunities along the lines of race and poverty, conflict with the very value systems that provide ideological impulse to the effort.

For these reasons, English composition, language arts, and literacy teachers who hope to address some of the inequities associated with the national effort to expand technological literacy in more productive ways may find the task a difficult one. Other teachers, parents, administrators, politicians, and students who do not have a critical perspective on the technology-literacy link, in general, or who have not studied the effects, more specifically, of the Technology Literacy Challenge may neither recognize the need for change nor condone efforts to alter the current situation.

Part Three

The Future and Our Responsibility:
Sites and Plans for Action and Change

8 / Paying Attention to Technology, Learning about Literacy

The experience of Virtually Wired and other urban computer centers suggests that the gap between high-end users of computer information and the information "have nots" could be much wider than thought.

"We found that there really is a wide degree of computer . . . illiteracy out there that cuts across all class lines," adds Mr. [Chris] Lee, treasurer of Virtually Wired.

Not only the poor and the homeless are being excluded. The growing economic gap between rich and poor in the U.S., according to the U.S. Department of Labor, means many Americans with declining incomes have less access to computers. . . .

A 1995 study by the Rand Corporation concluded that as more U.S. commercial and government transactions take place online, fewer Americans will participate if barriers of income, race, residential location, and age persist. (Holstrom 14)

Reflecting and Acting on the Technology and Literacy Link

The previous chapters have presented only a partial snapshot of the complex and articulated cultural formations that link technology and literacy in America and give specific shape to the Technology Literacy Challenge, the national project to expand technological literacy. Even this incomplete picture, however, illustrates the overdetermined nature of the connection between technology and literacy and suggests how effectively this link resonates with cultural values and beliefs. From this perspective, the picture describes an exceedingly difficult environment for teachers who want to make changes.

And yet, having read these chapters, teachers of English, composition, and language arts may also find it equally difficult—even professionally irresponsible or shameful—to ignore the national project to expand technological literacy, to ignore the serious social inequities associated with this project, including the uneven distribution of technologies along the lines of both race and socioeconomic status, the continuing reproduction of both illiteracy and poverty, and the differential educational opportunities accorded to students by virtue of their family income or their skin color.

So how do we undertake a process of making change? And where can we begin? Most teachers start small, often by identifying some immediate or local social, political, economic, or educational problem. This initial critical consciousness, in turn, provides the impulse to act, often in the context of one program, one classroom, an assignment, a community, or a single personal interaction with a student and his or her family.

But acquiring a critical consciousness, starting on the path of reflection leading to action, is also difficult, especially in terms of technology or technological literacy. This is, after all, an area in which teachers may have little expertise or even interest.

It is this lack of familiarity with technology, however, that can provide the intellectual perspective we need to begin making changes. By *paying attention* to the unfamiliar subject of technology—in sustained and critical ways, and from our own perspectives as humanists—we may learn some important lessons about how to go about making change in literacy instruction. Moreover, in the specific lessons we learn within the context of our own professional and personal expertise, we may be able to locate personal beginning points for initiating change.

As a starting point, I offer four lessons drawn from the specific case study of technological literacy.

Lesson #1: Remembering the Truth about Large-Scale Literacy Projects and the Myth of Literacy

The first lesson that the national project to expand technological literacy can teach us has to do with the efficacy of large-scale literacy projects and with the "literacy myth" (Graff 1991).

One of the primary arguments for the project to expand technological literacy rests on the claim that such an effort will provide all Americans with an education enriched by technology and thus equal opportunity to obtain high-paying, technology-rich jobs and economic prosperity after graduation. The truth of this claim, however, has not been borne out and is not likely to be so. This is one reason why we need to pay attention to technology issues.

Scholars such as Brian Street, Harvey Graff, and James Paul Gee note that such claims are not unusual in connection with large-scale national literacy projects. Indeed, our willingness to believe these claims contributes to the potency of the "literacy myth" (Graff 1991), the widely held belief that literacy and literacy education lead autonomously, automatically, and directly to liberation, personal success, or economic prosperity. This myth, however, is delusory in its simplicity, as Street says:

> The reality [of national literacy movements] is more complex, is harder to face politically. . . . [T]he level of literacy is less important than issues of class, gender, and ethnicity; lack of literacy is more likely to be a symptom of poverty and deprivation than a cause. (18)

In the specific case of the project to expand technological literacy, the claim is that the Technology Literacy Challenge will offer all citizens equal access to an improved education and thus equal opportunity for upward social mobility and economic prosperity. If we pay attention to the facts surrounding the project's instantiation, however, we can remind ourselves of the much harder lesson: in our educational system, and in the culture that this system reflects, computers continue to be distributed differentially along the related axes of race and socioeconomic status, and this distribution contributes to ongoing patterns of racism and to the continuation of poverty.

Acknowledging these facts, we might understand better why the rhetoric associated with national literacy projects serves to exacerbate the dangers that they pose. When Secretary of Education Richard Riley states, for example, that computers are the "new basics" of education or that the project of technological literacy can help us give "all of our young people" an opportunity to "grow and thrive" in the "new knowledge- and information-driven economy" (*Getting America's Students Ready* 3), he erroneously suggests, in Brian Street's words, "that the acquisition of literacy" will, "in itself, 'autonomously' lead to 'major' impacts in terms of social and cognitive skills and 'Development'" within a population (13).

As Street reminds us, these "simple stories" that "both politicians and the press" tell about literacy to justify and sustain the momentum of such major programs frequently "deflect attention from the complexity and real political difficulties" of literacy instruction. The ultimate effect of such stories, according to Street, is an overly narrow understanding of literacy—usually in terms of a single official literacy—and the development of accompanying "patronizing assumptions about what it means to have difficulties with reading and writing in contemporary society; and the raising of false hopes about what the acquisition of literacy means for job prospects, social mobility and personal achievement" (17).

In the specific case of technological literacy, these stories serve to deflect our attention from the fact that "every single child" (*Getting America's Students Ready* 4) does not have access to technology, and some students, especially those who are poor and of color, have less access than others. And so, if access to and use of technology in school-based settings is now a fundamental skill of literacy, as Riley suggests, and if such skills do help prepare graduates for the jobs they will be asked to do, these same students can expect fewer opportunities to assume high-tech and high-paying jobs, not more.

The frustrating cycle associated with this situation is so dismally clear and sickeningly familiar because it mirrors exactly the dynamics associated with more traditional literacy efforts in our country. As Graff (1987) notes, official literacies usually function in a conservative and reproductive fashion in favor of dominant groups and in support of the existing class-based system:

> Hegemonic relationships have historically involved processes of group and class formation, recruitment, indoctrination, and maintenance at all levels of society. For most of

> literacy's history, these functions have centered upon elite
> groups and their cohesion and power. For them, the uses
> of literacy have been diverse, but have included com-
> mon education, culture, and language . . . ; shared inter-
> ests and activities; control of scarce commodities, such
> as wealth, power, and even literacy; and common symbols
> and badges, of which literacy could be one. (12)

Thus, the national project to expand technological literacy has
not served to reduce illiteracy or the persistent social problems that
exacerbate illiteracy. Rather, it has simply changed the official criteria for the labels of both "literate" and "illiterate" while retaining
the basic ratio of individuals in both groups.

In sum, there exists little evidence that any large-scale project
focusing on a narrowly defined set of officially sanctioned literacy
skills will result in fundamental changes in the ratio of people labeled as *literate* or *illiterate*. These categories are socially constructed identities which our current educational system repro-
duces rather than addresses. Similarly, there is no specific evidence
that the current project to expand technological literacy will change
the patterns of literacy and illiteracy in this country. Rather, this
project is likely to support persistent patterns of economically
based literacy acquisition because citizens of color and those from
low socioeconomic backgrounds continue to have less access to
high-tech education and to occupy fewer high-paying positions that
make multiple uses of technology than do white citizens or those
from higher socioeconomic backgrounds.

Lesson #2: Literacy Education Is a Political Act

Given the effects just described, the national project to expand
technological literacy teaches a second lesson: that literacy is always a political act as well as an educational effort. In this context,
the Technology Literacy Challenge can be understood to be an effort motivated as much by political and economic agendas as it was
by educational values and goals.

The Clinton-Gore administration's role in formulating this national project provides a concrete example. The administration attempted to revitalize a flagging domestic economy and address America's diminished role as an effective international player in global marketplaces and political arenas.

The domestic engine of technology had to be cranked up, and to accomplish this goal, the administration knew that it had to accomplish two tasks:

- Educate a pool of technologically sophisticated workers and technology specialists who could reach new global markets and export more American manufactured equipment and specialized technology services to the rest of the world; and
- Provide an influx of resources into the domestic computer industry so that it could simultaneously support the international effort and assume an increasingly important role in revitalizing the American domestic economy.

And it was in response to these economic and political goals that the national project to expand technological literacy was born.

The dynamics that underlie the Technology Literacy Challenge were ideally and specifically suited to these economic and political goals. Touted as an educational effort designed to improve citizens' literacy levels and thus their opportunities for future prosperity, the project was targeted at producing a continuing supply of educated workers who had the skills necessary to design and manufacture increasingly sophisticated technological goods and could offer specialized technological services in international arenas.

Moreover, such a plan was pretty close to self-fueling. Students who learned the habits of reading, writing, and communicating on computers in school would tend to buy and use such goods after graduation, thus injecting a continuous flow of money into the computer industry.

And the plan's effects in the public sector promised to resonate with its effects in the private sector: when citizens were exposed to cutting-edge technologies at work or in school, they would desire them in their homes and they would purchase updated technologies more frequently. To ensure the continuation of the same high-tech careers and industries that have served them so well, such citizens would also tend to vote in support of political and economic programs that involved the further expansion of technology markets both domestically and internationally. Moreover, they would recognize the key role that technological literacy plays in their own success and so demand a similar education for their children.

A darker side of this dynamic is also evident. The economic engine of technology has produced not only a continuing supply of individuals who are highly literate in terms of technological knowledge but also an ongoing supply of individuals who fail to acquire technological literacy, those who are termed *illiterate* according to the official definition. These latter individuals provide the unskilled, inexpensive labor necessary to sustain the system just described; they generate the surplus labor that must be continually reinvested in capital projects to produce more sophisticated technologies.

As expected, the people described as illiterate in connection with technology are those with the least power to effect a change in this system. They come from families who attend the poorest schools in this country, and they attend schools with the highest black and Hispanic populations. As students, they have less access to sophisticated technology. As a result, they are hired into less desirable, lower-paid positions that demand fewer official technological literacy skills and pay lower wages.

Moreover, because skills in technological communication environments are so closely linked with literacy instruction in general and because students who come from such backgrounds are afforded the poorest efforts of the educational system and the lowest expectations of many teachers, the label of *illiterate* has broader implications for these individuals' ability to acquire other skills through their formal schooling years.

Lesson #3: Acquiring a Technological Understanding of the World

The project to expand technological literacy can help us relearn a philosophical lesson as well: the danger of understanding technol-

ogy as a solution for larger social, educational, political, and economic problems.

The difficulties associated with this approach are outlined in
Martin Heidegger's treatise *The Question Concerning Technology*. In
this work, Heidegger dwells not on technology itself but, rather, on
those problems caused by the relationship that humans establish
with technology, specifically, the very human habit of understanding the world as a series of problems that are amenable to technological fixes. Heidegger sees this way of thinking as a *technological
understanding* of the world, and he identifies it as particularly problematic because it forces humans into positions of dependence:

> [T]he essence of technology is by no means anything tech-
> nological. Thus we shall never experience our relationship
> to the essence of technology so long as we merely conceive
> and push forward the technological, put up with it, or
> evade it. Everywhere, we remain unfree and chained to
> technology whether we passionately affirm or deny it. But
> we are delivered over to it in the worst possible way when
> we regard it as something neutral. (4)

When humans have a technological understanding of the
world, we see technology in a very narrow way: as a tool for solving problems, as a means to an end. When mass housing becomes
a problem, for example, multifloored residences are proposed as a
way of accommodating more people cheaply in a single site. When
energy consumption is identified as a problem, a series of dams and
plants are designed and built to provide hydroelectric and nuclear
power. When disease is identified as a problem, x-ray machines and
magnetic resonance imagers are invented. When space exploration
becomes a problem, probes, orbiting telescopes, and robots are created to undertake the preliminary steps of exploration. Heidegger
writes,

> The current conception of technology, according to which
> it is a means and a human activity, can therefore be called

the instrumental and anthropological definition of technology. . . . [T]echnology [becomes] . . . a man-made means to an end. (5)

As humans adopt this "instrumental" understanding of technology, we also begin to think that all problems can be solved with technology and that the newest technology is all we need to master the natural environment as well:

Everything depends on our manipulating technology in the proper manner as a means. . . . We will master it. The will to mastery becomes all the more urgent the more technology tends to slip from human control. (5)

Such a view is dangerous, Heidegger asserts, for at least two reasons. First, it encourages us to understand and experience the world as a series of problems amenable to technological fixes. Equally as problematic, perhaps, this technological understanding of the world encourages the intellectual habit of perceiving everything around us, including the natural world, as a "standing-reserve" (17) of resources that can be used to create, design, and manufacture technologies.

As we develop these two related intellectual habits, Heidegger notes further, we begin the process of ordering the world, and everything in it, to the service of technology. Through this process of ordering the world, man "ensnares nature as an area of his own conceiving" and as an "object of research" (19). This mind-set blinds us to a full understanding of the natural world as well as a full understanding of our relationship to this world and to the technology we have created. This way of "enframing" the world (20) becomes dangerous when it limits our repertoire of response to a "single way" (32) and when our other ways of understanding the world atrophy and disappear.

Even worse, Heidegger points out, when we fall into the habit of ordering the world's resources into a standing reserve at our personal disposal, without realizing it we can even come "to the very brink" of seeing other humans as part of this standing reserve, as objects to be put to the service of technology. In this sense, we fail to understand ourselves as "the one spoken to" (27) by our limited understanding of technology and our relationship to it.

Within this context, the national project to expand technological literacy can be understood as an attempt to provide a technological fix for many social, political, educational, and economic problems. As a nation, we perceive a series of problems: a flagging domestic economy, the loss of prestige as a world leader after the cold war, persistent poverty, differential educational and economic opportunities based on race, and sagging test scores. Influenced by what Heidegger might identify as a habitual technological understanding of the world, we watch as national leaders identify a "solution": the economic engine of technology, developed and deployed both domestically and internationally.

This solution is explained as a way of addressing the country's needs in a global marketplace, the needs of business on a domestic front, and the economic prosperity of individuals. Citizens respond by helping to order the resources of the country in the service of this solution, making available the financial, political, and human resources required to build the NII and the GII (to provide outlets for expanded technology production) and to launch an expanded national project of technological literacy (to fuel industry's need for specialized labor and to build a domestic consumer market for more technology). And those who are a part of this system are thus incorporated into the service of technology.

Such a technological solution does not, of course, address the continuing problems associated with identifying and privileging a single official form of literacy. Nor does it address the continuing reproduction of the literacy/illiteracy split that results from such an arrangement in the case of technological literacy.

Lesson #4: Recognizing Our Own Role in Technological Literacy and the Literacy/Illiteracy Cycle

A fourth lesson derived from studying the national project to expand technological literacy has to do with our own role in the project and the recognition that our actions as teachers usually have unplanned and contradictory results, despite our best intentions.

As I indicated in chapter 1, teachers of English, composition, and language arts are generally content with the culture's traditional separation of arts and technology. This separation rests on a powerful set of ideological beliefs that establishes a gap between science and art, between scientists and humanist scholars, and this gap has structured Western culture for much of its history (Latour). The separation has also served to structure the responsibilities of English studies professionals in some very comfortable ways. Operating within the context of its particular common sense, we can use technology in our classrooms while generally absolving ourselves from the responsibility for planning for technology, thinking critically about technology, systematically assessing the value of technology, and making the difficult decisions associated with who pays for and has access to technology (see R. Selfe; Selfe and Selfe; Hawisher and Selfe 1993).

This separation has also allowed us to ignore the national project to expand technological literacy as a coherent, nationally funded literacy project. In this specific case, the very word *technology* has given us a sufficient excuse for professional inattention. This situation persists even though literacy teachers at all levels have been broadly affected by this official project for the past five years (and many times involved in various areas of it) and will continue to be so involved well into the next century. It persists despite the effects of this large-scale literacy project: the continuing reproduction of illiteracy in our culture along the related axes of race and poverty. In Eagleton's words, the belief system that provides the foundation for this separation has rendered its assumptions so "natural and self-evident" that they now correspond with common sense in our culture and "nobody can imagine how they might ever be different" (58).

Most ironically of all, it is within this effectively naturalized matrix of interests that English teachers have become the unwitting purveyors of technology and technological literacy, even as we try to avoid a technological focus by attending to more traditionally conceived topics within the humanities.

The paradoxical dynamics at the heart of this situation are difficult to understand because they function at so many levels. Because teachers fail to address the project to expand technological literacy systematically within the professional arenas available to us, we have come to understand technology as "just another instructional tool" that we can choose either to use or to ignore. Working from this context, we divide ourselves into two *meaningless* camps: those who use computers to teach classes and those who don't.

Both groups feel virtuous about their choices, and both manage to lose sight of the real issue: how to use technology, or relate to it, in ways that are productive and meaningful. The teachers who use computers guide students in using technology. But, all too often, they neglect to teach students how to pay critical attention to the issues generated by technology use, to help students develop a *critical technological literacy* (see chapter 9). The teachers who choose not to use computers in their classes mistakenly believe that their choice to avoid computers absolves them and their students from paying critical attention to technology issues. In other words, both groups contribute to the very same end.

And when such things happen, when we allow ourselves to ignore technological issues, when we take technology for granted, when it becomes *invisible* to us, when we forget technology's material bases—regardless of whether or not we use technology—we participate *unwittingly* in the inequitable literacy system I have just described.

Toward Action

As Bruno Latour notes, real-life stories always lack richness and accuracy when they are told from a single perspective. We require multiple perspectives if we hope to construct a robust and accurate understanding of the ways in which technology functions in our culture, especially within the context of literacy practices and values. Our profession's occasional respectful attention to technology and the social issues that surround technology may allow us to see things from a slightly different point of view, even if for only a moment. And from such a perspective, as Latour reminds us, our interpretations of issues "take on added density" (viii).

This occasional merging of the technological and the humanist perspectives into a vision that is more robustly informed has as much value for scientists and engineers as it does for humanists. Margaret Boden, an early pioneer in artificial intelligence, notes in the introduction to her 1977 landmark book that she was drawn to the study of artificial intelligence for its potential in "counteracting the dehumanizing influence of natural science" and for its ability to "clarify the nature of human purpose, freedom, and moral choice," those "hidden complexities of human thinking" (4), which machines cannot replicate, that have always concerned us most within this profession.

9 / Working for Change

Wiring the schools will not save them. The problems with America's public schools—disparate funding, social promotion, bloated class size, crumbling infrastructure, lack of standards—have almost nothing to do with technology. Consequently, no amount of technology will lead to the educational revolution prophesied by President Clinton and others. The art of teaching cannot be replicated by computers, the Net, or by "distance learning."

... Understanding technology should be an essential component of global citizenship. In a world driven by the flow of information, the interfaces—and the underlying code—that make information visible are becoming enormously powerful social forces. Understanding their strength s and limitations, and even participating in the creation of better tools, should be an important part of being an involved citizen. These tools affect our lives as much as laws do, and we should subject them to a similar democratic scrutiny. (Bennehum et al. 20)

[I]n thinking of the mechanisms of power, I am thinking rather of its capillary form of existence, the point where power reaches into the very grain of individuals, touches their bodies, and inserts itself into their actions and attitudes, their discourses, learning processes and everyday lives. (Foucault 39)

Situated Knowledges and Technological Literacy:
The Individual and Collective Arts of Paying Attention

So how do teachers deal more productively with technological literacy? Where do they begin to address the issues identified in the preceding chapters?

146

The primary factors determining any individual's involvement, of course, necessarily starts with the local and specific: social agents' own deep and penetrating knowledge (Giddens) of the specific schools, districts, colleges, and universities in which they work; the particular families, communities, and cultures within which they live and form their own understanding of the world; the individual students, teachers, administrators, board members, politicians, and parents whose lives touch their own.

This local "situated knowledges" approach to paying attention to the technology-literacy link is a kind of "coyote" way of knowing, in Donna Haraway's terms, one different from the traditional perspective of Science, but capable of offering a "more adequate, richer, better account of the world" that makes it possible to "live in it well and in critical, reflexive relation to our own as well as others' practices" (178). Such an approach, when substituted for the more traditional coherent vision claimed by Science or Research, may provide "only partial perspective," Haraway cautions (181), but it allows us to avoid the trap of claiming a scientific objectivity that invites a false sense of closure and simplistic answers.

If teachers pay attention to technology and literacy problems on a local level, they can collectively work to construct a larger vision of these issues on a professional level. These bits of knowledge about literacy practices in electronic environments, which individual teachers assemble for our profession, can be "stitched together imperfectly" (Haraway 183) to form a picture of technological literacy as it now functions within the American culture, one that might allow us to act with more strategic effectiveness and force, both collectively and individually.

This kind of situated-knowledges approach to paying attention also honors a multiplicity of responses to technological literacy. Given the constraints of local and specific contexts, and a commitment to engaging with the lives of individual students, for example, some teachers will work best alone; others will be more effective working with colleagues. Some educators will find work within their own classroom to be the most pressing effort, and others will find the action in local communities to offer the most immediate and successful venue for their work. Indeed, recognizing local situations and variations can help us appreciate the power of large-scale projects when they are built on the critical understandings and active participation of a diverse group of educators.

A theme that informs and shapes efforts in all the sites that follow—and a possible direction for an informed professional approach to the technology issues outlined in this book—involves an important transformation of the term *technological literacy* into the term *critical technological literacy*.

The term *technological literacy*, as noted in chapter 1, refers to the complex set of socially and culturally situated values, practices, and skills involved in operating linguistically within the context of electronic environments, including reading, writing, and communicating. The transformed term, *critical technological literacy*, suggests a reflective awareness of these social and cultural phenomena. Building on the work of literacy scholars like Street, Gee, and Graff, the use of critical technological literacy suggests a political agenda. Literate citizens should be able to carefully analyze, to pay attention to, the technology-literacy link at fundamental levels of both conception and social practice. Citizens are also responsible for understanding the social and cultural contexts for on-line discourse and communication, the social and linguistic products and practices of technological communication, and the ways in which electronic communication environments have become linked to literacy instruction.

Sites for Social Action Based on Situated Knowledges and Paying Attention

Operating from an understanding of the local and particular, suggestions for a critical engagement with technological literacy issues must allow for wide variations in social, political, economic, and ideological goals, as well as wide variations in teachers, students, administrators, citizens, and communities. In deference to this approach, the suggestions that follow focus on just a few of the most obvious sites for informed action and the development of critical technological literacy. Teachers, students, parents, and school administrators must determine within such sites how best to focus on the link between technology and literacy, recognizing that the local conditions will affect their purposes and the work they can accomplish.

In curriculum committees, standards documents, and assessment programs, teachers need to steadfastly resist projects and systems that serve to establish one narrow, official version of literacy practices or skills. Such projects and systems simply serve to reward the literacy practices of dominant groups and punish the practices of others. They serve to reproduce a continuing and oppressive cycle of illiteracy, racism, and poverty in this country and elsewhere. Within the venues of curriculum committees, program documents, and assessment efforts, we should insist on a diverse range of literacy practices and values.

Individual writing programs and English departments can also place a value on multiple literacies. Computers should *not* be required in every course, or teachers should decide when and where a range of technological *and* nontechnological literacies should be taught—and not taught—in a curriculum. Faculty should also decide how technological literacies are to be presented and assessed in comparison with other literacies. And faculty should explain their goals to students, administrators, parents, and colleagues.

In these sites, we also need to mention critical technological literacy. We have begun this effort by defining critical technological literacy in the standards document of the NCTE (*Standards for the English Language Arts*), but in the CCCCs we need to go much further. We need to help both future teachers and those already in classrooms understand why this work is so important and what implications their successes and failures may have.

In professional organizations, teachers need to recognize that if written language and literacy practices are their professional business, so is technology—and so is critical technological literacy. On a practical level, this recognition demands a series of carefully considered and very visible professional stands on various technological issues now under debate: for example, on the basic requirements for technological access, the direction and use of technology funding for schools, on how best to provide multiple venues for students' literacy practices, and on how best to shape the national project to expand technological literacy. Literacy teachers need to engage in more professional activism on these issues.

Current efforts by professional organizations provide a starting place. The Modern Language Association, for example, has published guidelines for "Evaluating Computer-Related Work in the Modern Languages." The National Council of Teachers of English Conference on College Composition and Communication has begun work in this area. However, given the ideological potency of both the Science-Humanities schism and the technology-literacy link, the increasing effectiveness of such work is likely to demand the collaborative interaction of multiple professional organizations that have been content to operate in separate spheres. Teachers can exert additional pressures on their professional organizations to undertake collective work.

Working in collaboration with the International Reading Association and the College English Association, for example, the MLA and NCTE might identify a collective set of standards for technological resource allocation and for levels of technology access in public schools. Similarly, these organizations might work together to arrive at a broadly acceptable definition of critical technological literacy. Collaborative projects might also help professional organizations agree on the best role of technological literacy in the context of the multiple literacies that children and adults need to acquire. Productive collaborative projects might also cross disciplinary boundaries to involve professional societies in mathematics, sciences, and engineering in an even larger process of defining the scope and value of critical technological literacy.

Professional organizations like the NCTE, CCCC, or MLA can also assume some of the responsibility for offering members resources for developing critical perspectives on technological literacy. The CCCC, for example, has recently funded a Technology Center in the exhibit area of their annual convention. Its goal is to give all members basic access to technology and technology issues related to their professional field. The Technology Center also offers information about developing critical perspectives on technological literacy; resources for professional and political action on literacy projects and legislation; instruction in technology use; and examples of meaningful technology integration in English, composition, and language arts programs.

Professional organizations can assume additional responsibility for helping faculty develop critical perspectives on technological literacy by suggesting guidelines for teacher preparation programs and in-service programs that include elements of technology criticism and technology education.

In scholarship and research efforts, teachers need to recognize that developing an increasingly critical perspective on technological literacy and technology issues is a responsibility of our profession as well as that of scientists and engineers. So we might undertake more research into technological literacy, including large-scale statistical surveys of technology distribution in English, composition, language arts, and literacy classrooms; small-scale institutional studies comparing technological literacy expectations in English with those in other disciplines; qualitative studies of how technology is being integrated into classrooms at various grade levels; linguistic analyses of on-line reading and writing practices on the World Wide Web; interpretive examinations of the ideological systems and cultural formations that currently inform the literacy-technology link; or studies of the historical patterns established by other technologies used in literacy classrooms. We might examine the effects that technological literacies have on students' attitudes toward other literacies, on parents' and school districts' definitions of student success, on documents that combine visual and written literacy, and on student confidence.

An important contribution of studies completed by English, composition, language arts teacher-researchers might be a rich blend of social, political, and economic perspectives that helps constitute an increasingly robust and critical understanding of technological literacy as an educational and cultural phenomenon. Regina Copeland, for example, has studied student technology access and use in eleven high schools in West Virginia. She focused on the access that students of color, poor students, and young women have had to computer-supported literacy instruction, the sophistication of the technology to which each of these groups has access, and expenditures by governments, schools, and families in support of technology and literacy.

Similarly, in 1998, at California State University in Los Angeles, Nancy Guerra Barron examined the relationship between technology and the situated literacy practices of Latino students, indicating how teachers might use technology to support a wider range of literacy goals for different populations. In particular, she examined the bilingual on-line discussions of Latino students in a Chicano studies class and traced the ways in which these students managed to shape and use electronic environments productively to mirror the linguistic richness of their lives outside the classroom.

These research efforts represent only two of the many that our profession needs to encourage.

In language arts and English studies classrooms and in first-year and advanced English composition courses, teachers need to recognize that they can no longer simply educate students to become technology consumers without also helping them learn how to think critically about technology and the social issues surrounding its use. When we require students to use computers in completing assignments, without also giving them the opportunity to explore the complex social and cultural issues that surround technology, we may be contributing to the education of citizens who use technology but who do not understand the complex relationships between humans, machines, and the contexts within which they interact.

Composition and language arts teachers and other literacy specialists need to recognize that the relevance of technology in English studies is not simply a matter of helping students learn to work effectively with communication software and hardware. It is also a matter of helping them to understand and be able to assess the social, economic, and pedagogical implications of new communication technologies and the technological initiatives that directly and indirectly affect their lives. To develop this critical technological literacy, knowledgeable literacy specialists at all levels need to develop age-appropriate and level-appropriate reading and writing activities.

Anne Wysocki at Michigan Technological University, for example, has designed a writing assignment that encourages students to examine the actual costs and trade-offs inherent in technology decisions. This basic information is frequently invisible to students, who lack involvement in budgetary planning for computing resources. Because they do not ordinarily have such information available, many college students demand more technology, and more sophisticated technology on a continual basis, often without understanding what such a commitment might mean in terms of the diminution of other resources: lower salaries for student assistants, reduced access to basic computing for students, less frequent repair of existing technology, or upgrading of software.

In a course entitled Computer Applications in the Humanities, Wysocki hands students the annual budget of the department's computer-supported writing lab, a facility supported by student fees. The budget details what proportion of the fees collected is spent on new hardware and software, repairs to existing equipment, technical help, and salaries for student assistants. Students are asked to revise the budget according to their own goals with the caveat that their fiscal solution must have a balanced bottom line. Students are also asked to reflect on their decisions in writing. In the process of completing this assignment, students must weigh a number of considerations: Should they opt for more sophisticated technology purchases, but give less access to such purchases by fewer students? Should they sacrifice the salaries of the student workers employed in this facility in order to pay for additional computer stations? Should they limit software upgrades in order to pay for longer hours of operation? Do humanities majors need sophisticated new multimedia software at the expense of an upgraded word-processing capability for students from other majors?

Building this component of critical technological literacy into a communication or composition class is not difficult if a teacher is willing to work with students in authentic projects of classroom-based inquiry. Teachers could build writing and communication assignments around critical and systematic analyses of commercial images that portray computer use on television or in magazines; around student examinations of campus computing policies concerning harassment, pornography, or racism; around a systematic survey of how much it would cost a family of four to purchase and maintain on-line access in the surrounding community; around the allocation of computer resources in surrounding school districts or schools. Teachers could focus assignments in other ways as well to build in a critical component: asking students to analyze on-line class exchanges in order to compare the involvement of males and females, or native and nonnative English speakers; involving students in service-learning projects that provide computer instruction and access to populations without such access; and having students analyze statistics about the World Wide Web in terms of who does and does not have access to computers, both in and outside the United States.

In computer-based communication facilities, teachers need to identify practical ways of putting their scholarship and research to work in praxis—with the goal of supporting an increasingly critical perspective on technological literacy. Technology-rich facilities can serve not only as teaching environments for students completing critically oriented literacy assignments on-line, but also as sites within which students and faculty can formulate guidelines and policies that support critically informed practices and put these understandings to work in complicated social situations (R. Selfe).

Feenberg offers the possibility of considering such sites in terms of their *underdetermined* potential for political, economic, and social change—a potential which can be exploited by interested and knowledgeable social agents determined to make a difference. Technology-rich communication facilities are already replete with such interested agents: the teachers involved in designing and teaching within them, the students involved in using them and learning within them, the staff members (often students) responsible for keeping them operational, and the administrators who help to fund them.

In technology-rich communication facilities, these stakeholders can work collaboratively to address complex and contradictory technology problems and, in doing so, make a difference. Stakeholders, for example, can work collaboratively on one or more of the following thorny problems:

- Creating a set of scheduling priorities that will provide adequate access for faculty, classes, individual students, and technical staff members, all of whom have differing needs and goals for computer use.
- Identifying budgetary priorities that balance expenditures for teachers' technology needs with those of students, staff members, and administrators.
- Identifying the most appropriate balance between students' concern for increased access and their requests for more sophisticated machines.
- Setting an acceptable level for student lab fees and identifying work-for-pay schemes for students who cannot afford such fees.
- Deciding on on-line etiquette and guidelines that don't impinge on freedom of speech.

Such problems represent the complicated and often contradictory dilemmas that computer use introduces into academic settings. They are also part of the process of managing computer-supported communication environments, and they represent opportunities to establish a critical perspective on technology and compare stakeholders' needs. When a range of stakeholders can be involved in addressing such problems, decisions about technology use can be denaturalized, made increasingly visible and debatable. By virtue of this public process, decisions about technology become reconnected with the lived experiences of individuals (R. Selfe).

Finally, students and faculty who participate in such problem-solving projects can develop productive strategies of agency in connection with technology. In this regard, they acquire the habit of making critically informed decisions about technology rather than becoming passive consumers of technological goods. Our culture will need these activists in school board and PTO meetings, in small businesses, on corporate boards, and in government agencies where decisions about communication technologies will influence the personal and professional lives of citizens.

In states, districts, and systems that have poor schools, rural schools, and schools with large populations of students of color, teachers need to resist the forces that continue to link technological literacy with patterns of racism and poverty. One approach is to involve professional organizations in identifying a set of resource standards for technology use in literacy programs and to employ these standards to alert parents and literacy teachers to the dangers of differential technology funding and distribution.

In voting for school board elections, in committee meetings, in public hearings, at national conventions, in the public relations statements of professional organizations, teachers can argue that poor students and students of color should get increased access to computers and to more sophisticated computers, that teachers in schools with high populations of such students should be given additional support in terms of professional development.

At the state level, teachers can support legislation and educational projects that ensure an increasingly equitable distribution of technology. We can also lend our support to politicians who work to fund such projects. Virginia, Ohio, Illinois, Montana, South Dakota, and Pennsylvania have made some provisions for more equitable distribution in their technology plans for education.

In pre-service and in-service educational programs and curricula, we need to give colleagues the resources to develop an increasingly critical perspective on technological literacy. In rhetoric, composition, and English education graduate programs, we need to make sure that young professionals are not taught simply to *use* computers. Rather, they should be taught to pay critical attention to technology and the issues that result from, and contribute to, the technology-literacy link.

It is no longer enough, for instance, simply to ask graduate students or colleagues to use computers in the composition classes they teach or take. Instead, we need to help them read in the areas of technology criticism, social theory, and computer studies and allow them to develop critical technological literacy themselves. We also need to help graduate students plan assignments that will help undergraduates develop the same kind of critical perspectives on technological literacy.

To accomplish these goals, attention needs to be given to both pre-service and in-service work. This might include seminars on ways to integrate technology into specific English, composition, or language arts courses; professional development workshops on critical technical literacy; and reading groups on technology issues for graduate students and faculty.

At Michigan Tech, for example, humanities department faculty and graduate students can attend weekly seminars on teaching with technology. These seminars concern not only integrating computers appropriately into assignments for specific courses but also integrating a critical perspective on technology into courses that use technology. They also assist in locating readings on technological literacy to use with undergraduate students. Examples include Elisabeth Gerver's "Computers and Gender" (1989), Langdon Winner's "Mythinformation" (1986), Rob Glaser's "Universal Service Does Matter" (1995), Michael Apple's "The New Technology: Is It Part of the Solution or Part of the Problem in Education?" (1991), and Steven Silberman's "We're Teen, We're Queer, and We've Got E-Mail" (1994).

Teachers who work successfully with students and colleagues to develop approaches to critical technological literacy also need to describe such approaches in textbooks.

In libraries, community centers, and other nontraditional public places, literacy educators need to work for low-cost access to computers for citizens at the poverty level or citizens of color—not only so that such individuals have access to computers and thus can become proficient in computer use for communication tasks (Oppel) but also so that these citizens have access to the Internet and to on-line sites for collective political action (Hoffman and Novak).

To help equip such environments, teachers can seek grants, donations of used equipment and software, and commercial sponsorship support. To staff such efforts, faculty and graduate students can design service-learning projects into their literacy programs and courses, volunteer their time as literacy tutors or coaches, and encourage undergraduate students to participate as literacy assistants.

In such sites, teachers can volunteer to provide basic literacy instruction, conduct research, or identify web sites that would support collective political action.

In coalitions of teachers formed across grade levels—operating either locally or, via computer networks, at a distance—we can work together to examine our assumptions about technology use and the strategies and techniques we can employ to encourage critical technological literacy at all levels. College instructors can learn a great deal from secondary and elementary teachers about the developmental processes involved in acquiring literacies and about the ways in which we can value multiple literacies that students bring with them from home. Secondary and elementary teachers can learn what college-level teachers are seeking in terms of critical perspectives on language and technological literacy. Teachers at all levels can combine their expertise to influence educational policy, state standards, and classroom practices.

One example of such a venue is the annual summer institute for Computers in Writing Intensive Classrooms at Michigan Tech. In this two-week intensive seminar, American teachers and teachers from abroad exchange ideas on how to develop their own and students' critical technological literacy. Teachers not only get hands-on experience in using technology. They also are asked to examine their technology choices in light of their instructional goals, to analyze hardware and software decisions within the contexts of what they know about teaching and learning literacy, to study critical theories about technology, and to explore their own technologically based literacy practices and how they shape teaching, learning, and communication. Many of the cross-level discussions and alliances begun at this institute are continued on-line in various e-mail exchanges and listservs.

In coalitions of teachers and scholars working across geopolitical borders, we need to think critically about the effects of technology on a global scale, recognizing that the situation we know about in the United States may be only one manifestation of a much larger social formation. As Manuel Castells (1997) points out, the rise of the information society, the "pervasive, interconnected, and diversified media system" (1) that electronically links people around the world, has transformed the material foundations of labor, the formation of personal identity, and the nature of both time and space in fundamental ways. This transformation, Castells (1998) adds, has supported expansion of multinational capitalism and has contributed to the increase of both poverty and "extreme poverty" (133) in some countries or regions, including Africa and U.S. inner cities that have high populations of people of color. As Castells (1996) argues, it is the effects of "differential timing in access to the power of technology" that has served as "a critical source of inequality" for "people, countries, and regions" around the world and a factor in low levels of literacy and insufficient educational opportunities (34).

If we have the strength to recognize the links among technology, literacy, racism, and poverty in America, we can form transnational coalitions to discuss such observations with teachers from other countries. And we can then bring these discussions to the attention of families, social groups, professional societies, and governments. Coalitions of teachers can be formulated at a distance, using the very technology that has helped create such problems, or in face-to-face settings at international conferences sponsored by professional organizations like the International Federation of Teachers of English or the International Reading Association. Additionally, teachers and scholars can take advantage of teacher-exchange opportunities sponsored by professional societies to study the global effects of the technology-literacy linkage firsthand, and then to bring these observations to the attention of the larger educational community.

Toward an End . . .

Mark Weiser has said, "The most profound technologies are those that disappear," that "weave themselves into the fabric of everyday life until they are indistinguishable from it" (94). This may well be true. Technologies may be the most profound when they disappear. But when this happens, they also develop the most potential for being dangerous.

We have seen the twin strands of technology and literacy become woven into the fabric of our lives. They are now inscribed in legislation, in the warp and woof of our culture. Recognizing this context, however, we have an even greater responsibility to keep sight of both formations. We must remind ourselves that laws write the texts of people's lives, that they constantly inscribe their intent and power on individuals. As Michel de Certeau says, "There is no law that is not inscribed on bodies. Every law has a hold on the body. . . . It engraves itself on parchments made from the skin of its subjects. It articulates them in a juridical corpus. It makes its book out of them" (139–40).

It is our obligation, as educators, to commit ourselves to reading and analyzing these texts and the lives of students—honestly, with respect, and to the very best of our abilities. The alternative—of ignoring them, of perceiving students only in terms of their numbers in our schools or as undifferentiated members of groups—is simply unacceptable.

As Elspeth Stuckey, Mike Rose, Harvey Graff, Brian Street, James Paul Gee, and many others have told us, when we participate in unthinking ways in political agendas, legislative initiatives, or educational systems that support a very narrow version of official literacy, we all lose, and we are all implicated in the guilt that accrues to a system of violence through literacy.

Literacy professionals and the organizations that represent them need to commit to understanding the complex relationship between literacy and technology and to intervening in the national project to expand technological literacy. We must also realistically appraise the multiple roles that literacy educators are already playing in support of this project.

We need to acknowledge the economic and political goals that policymakers have identified as the end product of technology expansion: the effort to maintain and extend American privilege, influence, and power within an increasingly competitive global marketplace, ostensibly for the benefit of all citizens.

And literacy educators need to become increasingly hard-nosed about weighing the documented outcomes of the current project to expand technological literacy—the Technology Literacy Challenge—against the great expectations we continue to have as teachers: our belief that literacy instruction makes life more fulfilling, more clearly informed by democratic and humanistic values for the human beings we teach. Perhaps most important, we need to reconsider this national project in relation to our own work as literacy educators and citizens and in relation to our hopes for America's future.

It is my hope that by paying some attention to technology, we may become better humanists as well.

Works Cited

Index

Works Cited

Aley, James. 1995. "Where the Jobs Are." *Fortune*, 18 September, 53.

Apple, Michael. 1991. "The New Technology: Is It Part of the Solution or Part of the Problem in Education?" *Computers in the Schools* 8 (1–3): 59–77.

Aspen Institute Conference on Hispanic Americans and the Business Community. 1988. *Closing the Gap for U.S. Hispanic Youth: Public/Private Strategies.* 1988. Washington, D.C.: Hispanic Policy Development Project.

Baker, Eva L., and Harold F. O'Neill Jr., eds. 1994. *Technology Assessment in Education and Training.* Hillsdale, N.J.: Lawrence Erlbaum Associates.

Banks, Sandy, and Lucille Renwick. 1997. "Technology Remains Promise, Not Panacea; Education: Schools Have Invested Heavily, but with Little Academic Results. More Teacher Training Is Urged." *Los Angeles Times*, 8 June, A1.

Barron, Nancy Guerra. 1998. "Egalitarian Moments: Computer Mediated Communications in a Chicano Studies (ChS 111) Course." Master's thesis, California State University, Los Angeles.

Bell, Daniel. 1973. *The Coming of Post-Industrial Society: A Venture in Social Forecasting.* New York: Basic Books.

Bennehum, David S., Brooke S. Riggs, Paulina Borsook, Marissa Rowe, Simson Garfinkle, Steve Johnson, Douglas Rushkoff, Andrew L. Shapiro, David Shonk, Steve Silberman, Mark Stahlman, and Stephanie Syman. 1998. "Get Real! A Manifesto from a New Generation of Cultural Critics: Technorealism." *Nation*, 6 April, 19–20.

Berlin, James A. 1987. *Rhetoric and Reality: Writing Instruction in American Colleges, 1900–1985.* Carbondale: Southern Illinois University Press.

Birkerts, Sven. 1994. *Gutenberg Elegies: The Fate of Reading in an Electronic Age.* New York: Fawcett Columbine.

Blom, Eric. 1996. "It Clicks for Kids; Some Warn of Computer Overuse, and of Inequities in Access, But for the Most Part, They Say: Start 'Em Young." *Portland Press Herald*, 16 June, 1G.

Boden, Margaret. 1977. *Artificial Intelligence and Natural Man.* New York: Basic Books.

Bordieu, Pierre. 1977. *Outline of a Theory of Practice.* Cambridge: Cambridge University Press.

Braverman, Harry. 1974. *Labor and Monopoly Capital: The Degradation of Work in the Twentieth Century.* New York: Monthly Review Press.

Castells, Manuel. 1996. *The Rise of the Network Society.* Volume 1 of *The Information Age: Economy, Society, and Culture.* Malden, Mass.: Blackwell.

——. 1997. *The Power of Identity.* Volume 2 of *The Information Age: Economy, Society, and Culture.* Malden, Mass.: Blackwell.

——. 1998. *End of the Millenium.* Volume 3 of *The Information Age: Economy, Society, and Culture.* Malden, Mass.: Blackwell.

Cerf, Vinton G. 1991. "Networks." *Scientific American*, September, 72–81.

Chacon, Richard. 1996. "Politicians Turn Out for NetDay in Massachusetts: The '96 Election/Massachusetts/Day to Net Votes." *Boston Globe*, 27 October, B6.

Cole, Michael, and Peg Griffin. 1987. *Contextual Factors in Education: Improving Science and Mathematics Education for Minorities and Women.* Madison: Wisconsin Center for Education Research, University of Wisconsin.

Coley, R. J., J. Crandler, and P. Engle. 1997. *Computers and Classrooms: The Status of Technology in U.S. Schools.* Educational Testing Service, Policy Information Center. Princeton, N.J.: ETS.

Collier, Richard M. 1983. "Computerized Word Processing as an Aid to Revision Strategies." *College Composition and Communication* 34(2): 149–55.

Collins, A. 1991. "The Role of Computer Technology in Restructuring Schools." *Phi Delta Kappan* 73(1): 28–36.

The Condition of Education 1997. June 1997. National Center for Education Statistics, Office of Educational Research and Improvement. U.S. Department of Education. Washington, D.C.

Copeland, Regina. 1997. "Identifying Barriers to Computer-Supported Instruction." Ph.D. diss., West Virginia University, Morgantown.

Corson, Ross. 1982. "Computer Revolution." *Progressive*, September, 32, 34–36.

Cyganowski, Carol K. 1990. "The Computer Classroom and Collaborative Learning: The Impact on Student Writers." *Computers and Community: Teaching Composition in the Twenty-First Century.* Ed. C. Handa. Portsmouth, N.H.: Boynton/Cook Heinemann. 68–88.

Daiute, Colette. 1983. "The Computer as Stylus and Audience." *College Composition and Communication* 34(2): 134–45.

Davis, L. 1996. Logic Boards, Not Blackboards: The Schools' Low-Wire Act Leaves Students Dangling. *Dallas Observer*, 25 September.

de Certeau, Michel. 1984. *The Practice of Everyday Life.* Trans. Steven Randall. Berkeley: University of California Press.

Deloughry, Thomas J. 1994. "Unconnected." *Chronicle of Higher Education*, 23 February, A19–20.

Digest of Education Statistics 1996. November 1996. National Center for Educational Statistics, Office of Educational Research and Improvement, U.S. Department of Education. NCES 96-133.

Dubrovsky, Vitaly J., Sara Kiesler, and Beheruz N. Sethna. 1991. "The Equalization Phenomenon: Status Effects in Computer-Mediated and Face-to-Face Decision-Making Groups." *Human-Computer Interaction* 6:119–46.

Duin, Ann H., and Craig J. Hansen. 1996. *Nonacademic Writing: Social Theory and Technology.* Mahwah, N.J.: Lawrence Erlbaum Associates.

Duling, R. 1985. *Word Processors and Student Writing: A Study of Their Impact on Revision, Fluency, and Quality of Writing.* Ph.D. diss., Michigan State University.

Eagleton, Terry. 1991. *Ideology: An Introduction.* London: Verso.

Economic Report of the President. 1997. Council of Economic Advisers. February. Washington, D.C.: Government Printing Office.

"Evaluating Computer-Related Work in the Modern Languages." 1996. *Profession '96*, 217–19.

Evenson, Laura. 1997. "Seymour Papert: Computers in the Lives of Our Children." *San Francisco Chronicle*, 2 February, Z1, 3.

Faigley, Lester. 1997. "Literacy After the Revolution." *College Composition and Communication* 48(1): 30–43.

Falk, C. J. 1985. "English Skills Tutorials for Sentence Combining Practice." *Computers and Composition* 2(3): 2–4.

Feenberg, Andrew. 1991. *Critical Theory of Technology.* New York: Oxford University Press.

———. 1995. *Alternative Modernity: The Technical Turn in Philosophy and Social Theory.* Berkeley: University of California Press.

Foucault, Michel. 1980. *Power/Knowledge: Selected Interviews and Other Writings, 1972–1977.* Ed. Colin Gordon. Trans. Colin Gordon, Leo Marshall, John Mepham, and Kate Soper. New York: Pantheon Books.

Freeman, Laura. 1996. "Job Creation and the Emerging Home Computer Market." *Monthly Labor Review* 119 (August): 46–56.

Fuchs, I. A. 1983. "BITNET—Because It's Time." *Perspectives in Computing* 3(1): 16–27.

Gee, James Paul. 1990. *Social Linguistics and Literacies: Ideology in Discourses.* Brighton, U.K.: Falmer Press.

Geewax, Martin. 1996. "Internet Should Be Open to All." *Palm Beach Post*, 20 October, 6E.

Gellene, D. 1995. "At Some Back-to-School Nights, Apple Gets the Teachers; Marketing: The Computer Maker Is Enlisting Instructors to Plug Its Products. Critics Say It Compromises Schools." *Los Angeles Times*, 24 December, D3.

Gergen, Kenneth. 1991. "The Saturated Self." *Dilemmas of Identity in Contemporary Life.* New York: Basic Books.

Gerrard, Lisa. 1987. *Writing at Century's End: Essays on Computer-Assisted Composition.* New York: Random House.

Gerver, Elisabeth. 1989. "Computers and Gender." *Computers in the Human Context: Information Technology, Productivity, and People.* Ed. Tom Forester. Cambridge: Massachusetts Institute of Technology. 481–501.

Gessen, Masha. 1995. "Balkans Online." *Wired* 3(11): 158–62, 220–28.

Getting America's Students Ready for the Twenty-First Century: Meeting the Technology Literacy Challenge. A Report to the Nation on Technology and Education. 1996. Washington, D.C.: U.S. Department of Education.

Gibbons, J. 1993. Testimony by John H. Gibbons, director of the Office of Science Technology Policy before the Committee on Science, Space, and Technology of the U.S. House of Representatives. 27 April. News Statement from the Office of Science and Technology Policy at the White House. <http://www.whitehouse.gov/search/everything.html>

Giddens, Anthony. 1984. *The Constitution of Society: Outline of a Theory of Structuration.* Berkeley: University of California Press.

Gilbert, S. W., and D. P. Balestri. 1988. *Ivory Towers, Silicon Basements.* McKinney, Tex.: Academic Computing Publications.

Giroux, Henry. 1992. *Border Crossings: Cultural Workers and the Politics of Education.* New York: Routledge, Chapman, and Hall.

Giroux, Henry A., and Paulo Freire. 1987. "Series Introduction." *Critical Pedagogy and Cultural Power.* Ed. D. Livingstone. South Hadley, Mass.: Bergin and Garvey. xi–xvi.

"Give Your Child a Head Start for Life." 1997. Advertisement. *HomePC*, September, 175.

Glaser, Rob. 1995. "Universal Service Does Matter." *Wired* 3(1): 96–98.

Glennan, Thomas K., and Arthur Melmed. 1996. *Fostering the Use of Educational Technology: Elements of a National Strategy.* Santa Monica: Rand Corporation.

Global Information Infrastructure: Agenda for Cooperation. 1995. Issued by Al Gore, vice president of the United States, and Ronald H. Brown, secretary of commerce, Information Infrastructure Task Force, U.S. Department of Commerce. 31 January. Washington, D.C.: Government Printing Office.

Goals 2000: Increasing Student Achievement Through State and Local Initiatives. 30 April 1996. <http://www.ed.gov/G2K/GoalsRpt>

Goodman, William. 1996. "The Role of Computers in Reshaping the Work Force." *Monthly Labor Review* 119 (August): 37–45.

Gomez, Mary Louise. 1991. "The Equitable Teaching of Composition." *Evolving Perspectives on Computers and Composition Studies.* Ed. G. E. Hawisher and C. L. Selfe. Urbana, Ill., and Houghton, Mich.: National Council of Teachers of English and Computers and Composition Press. 318–35.

Gore, Albert. 1991. "Infrastructure for the Global Village." *Scientific American*, September, 150–53.

——. 1992. "The Information Infrastructure and Technology Act." *EDUCOM Review* 27 (September/October): 27–29.

——. 1993. Remarks to National Press Club, Washington, D.C. 21 December. <http://www.whitehouse.gov/search/everything.html>.

——. 1994. Speech to International Telecommunications Union in Buenos Aires, Argentina. 21 March. <http://www.whitehouse.gov/search/everything.html>

Graff, Harvey J. 1987. *The Legacies of Literacy: Continuities and Contradictions in Western Culture and Society.* Bloomington: Indiana University Press.

——. 1991. *The Literacy Myth: Cultural Integration and Social Structure in the Nineteenth Century.* New Brunswick, N.J.: Transaction.

Green, Kenneth C. 1996. "The Campus Computing Project." WWW site dated November 1996 and accessed 6 August 1998 at <http://ericir_syr.edu>.

"Guidelines for Evaluating Computer-Related Work in the Modern Languages." 1996. *Profession '96.* Guidelines issued by the Modern Language Association's Committee on Computers and Emerging Technologies, 217–19.

Handa, Carolyn, ed. 1990. *Computers and Community: Teaching Composition in the Twenty-First Century.* Portsmouth, N.H.: Boynton/Cook Heinemann.

Haraway, Donna. 1995. "Situated Knowledges: The Science Question in Feminism and the Privilege of Partial Perspective." *Technology and the Politics of Knowledge.* Ed. Andrew Feenberg and Alastair Hannay. Bloomington: Indiana University Press, 1995. 175–94.

Hardy, H. E. 1993. *USENET: The History of the Net.* Master's thesis (version 8.5), Grand Valley State University, Grand Valley, Mich. <http://vrx.net/usenet/thesis/hardy.html>.

Harris, Jeannette, and Joyce Kinkead. 1987. "Computers, Computers, Computers." Special issue of *Writing Center Journal* 8(1).

Harris, Muriel, and Madelon Cheek. 1984. "Computers Across the Curriculum: Using WRITER'S WORKBENCH for Supplementary Instruction." *Computers and Composition* 1(2): 3–5.

Harvey, J., ed. 1995. *Planning and Financing Educational Technology.* March. Washington, D.C.: Rand Corporation.

Hawisher, Gail E. 1988. "Research Update: Writing and Word Processing." *Computers and Composition* 5(2): 7–27.

——. 1989. "Research and Recommendations for Computers and Composition." *Critical Perspectives on Computers and Composition Instruction.* Ed. G. E. Hawisher and C. L. Selfe. New York: Teachers College Press. 44–69.

Hawisher, Gail E., and Paul LeBlanc. 1992. *Re-imagining Computers and Composition in the Virtual Age: Research and Teaching in the Virtual Age.* Portsmouth, N.H.: Boynton/Cook, Heinemann.

Hawisher, Gail E., Paul LeBlanc, Charles Moran, and Cynthia L. Selfe. 1996.

Computers and the Teaching of Writing in American Higher Education, 1979–1984: A History. Norwood, N.J.: Ablex.

Hawisher, Gail E., and Cynthia L. Selfe. 1989. *Critical Perspectives on Computers and Composition Instruction.* New York: Teachers College Press.

———. 1991. "The Rhetoric of Technology and the Electronic Writing Class." *College Composition and Communication* 42(1): 55–65.

———. 1993. "Tradition and Change in Computer-Supported Writing Environments: A Call for Action." *Theoretical and Critical Perspectives on Teacher Change.* Ed. P. Kahaney, J. Janangelo, and L. A. M. Perry. Norwood, N.J.: Ablex. 155–86.

Hawkins, J. 1985. "Computers and Girls: Rethinking the Issues." *Sex Roles* 13: 165–80.

Heidegger, Martin. 1977. *The Question Concerning Technology.* New York: Harper and Row.

Herrmann, Andrea. 1990. "Computers and Writing Research: Shifting Our 'Governing Gaze.'" *Computers and Writing: Theory, Research, Practice.* Ed. D. H. Holdstein and C. L. Selfe. New York: Modern Language Association. 124–34.

Hiltz, Starr R., and Murray Turoff. 1993. *The Network Nation: Human Communication via Computer.* Rev. ed. Cambridge: MIT Press.

Hispanic Policy Development Project. 1989. *Closing the Gap for U.S. Hispanic Youth: Public/Private Strategies.* Lanham, Md.: Aspen Institute and University Press of America.

Hoffman, Donna L., and Thomas P. Novak. 1998. "Bridging the Racial Divide on the Internet." *Science,* 17 April, 390–91.

Holdstein, Deborah. 1983. "The WRITEWELL Series." *Computers and Composition* 1(1): 7.

Holstrom, David. 1996. "Computer Centers Find Literacy Gap Persists." *Christian Science Monitor,* 30 July, 14 (Features).

HR 1804, Goals 2000: Educate America Act. 31 March 1994. <http://www.ed.gov/legislation/GOALS2000/TheAct>.

Jabs, Carolyn. 1997. "3 R's: Reading, 'Riting, and 'Rithmetic." *HomePC,* September, 105–16.

Jackson, Cheryl. 1997. "Blacks Must Be Computer Literate, TV Host Urges." *Tampa Tribune,* 26 June, Business and Finance, 1.

Jessup, Emily. 1991. "Feminism and Computers in Composition Instruction." *Evolving Perspectives on Computers and Composition Studies: Questions for the 1990s.* Ed. G. E. Hawisher and C. L. Selfe. Urbana, Ill., and Houghton, Mich.: National Council of Teachers of English and Computers and Composition Press. 336–55.

Jobst, John. 1984. "Computer-Assisted Grading of Essays and Reports." *Computers and Composition* 1(2): 5.

Johnson-Eilola, Johndan, and Stuart A. Selber. 1996. "After Automation: Hypertext and Corporate Structures." *Electronic Literacies in the Workplace: Technologies of Writing.* Ed. Patricia A. Sullivan and Jennie Dautermann. Urbana, Ill., and Houghton, Mich.: National Council of Teachers of English and Computers and Composition. 115–41.

Jones, B. F., G. Valdez, J. Nowakowski, and C. Rasmussen. 1995. *Plugging In: Choosing and Using Educational Technology.* Washington, D.C.: Council for Educational Development and Research.

Jones, Robert, Patrick Bizzaro, and Cynthia Selfe. 1997. *The Harcourt Brace Guide to Writing in the Disciplines.* Fort Worth, Tex.: Harcourt Brace.

Keltner, B. and Ross, B. 1995. *The Cost of High Technology Schools.* March. Washington, D.C.: Rand Corporation.

Kennedy, M. M., R. K. Jung, and M. E. Orland. 1986. *Poverty, Achievement, and the Distribution of Compensatory Education Services.* An interim report from the National Assessment of Chapter I, OERI. January. Washington, D.C.: Government Printing Office.

King, B., J. Birnbaum, and J. Wageman. 1984. "Word Processing and the Basic College Writer." *The Written Word and the Word Processor.* Ed. T. Martinez. Philadelphia: Delaware Valley Writing Council.

Klem, Elizabeth, and Charles Moran. 1992. "Teachers in a Strange LANd: Learning to Teach in a Networked Writing Classroom." *Computers and Composition* 9(3): 5–22.

Knoblauch, C. H. 1990. "Literacy and the Practice of Education." *The Right to Literacy.* Ed. Andrea A. Lunsford, Helen Moglen, and James Slevin. New York: Modern Language Association. 74–80.

Kobler, Ron. 1997. "Introducing Children to Computers." *Computing for Kids,* summer, 1.

Kulik, J. A. 1994. "Meta-Analytical Studies of Findings on Computer-Based Instruction." *Technology Assessment in Education and Training.* Ed. Eva L. Baker and Harold F. O'Neill Jr. Hillsdale, N.J.: Lawrence Album Associates.

Landow, George P. 1992. *The Convergence of Contemporary Critical Theory and Technology.* Baltimore: Johns Hopkins University Press.

———. 1994. *Hypertext Theory.* Baltimore: Johns Hopkins University Press.

Lanham, Richard. 1989. "The Electronic Word: Literary Study and the Digital Revolution." *New Literary History* 20(2): 265–90.

Latour, Bruno. 1996. *ARAMIS or the Love of Technology.* Trans. C. Porter. Cambridge: Harvard University Press.

LeBlanc, Paul. 1990. "Competing Ideologies in Software Design for Computer-Aided Composition." *Computers and Composition* 7(2): 8–19.

Livingstone, David, ed. 1987. *Critical Pedagogy and Cultural Power.* South Hadley, Mass.: Bergin and Garvey.

Lyotard, Jean-François. 1984. *The Postmodern Condition: A Report on Knowledge.*

Trans. Geoff Bennington and Brian Massumi. Minneapolis: University of Minnesota Press.

Marling, William. 1984. "Grading Essays on a Microcomputer." *College English* 46(8): 797–810.

McCann, Thomas M. 1984. "Sentence Combining for the Microcomputer." *Computers and Composition* 1(3): 1.

McConnell, Sheila. 1996. "The Role of Computers in Reshaping the Work Force." *Monthly Labor Review* 119 (August): 3–10.

McLuhen, Marshall. 1962. *The Gutenberg Galaxy: The Making of Typographic Man.* Toronto: University of Toronto Press.

Mead, Margaret. 1970. *Culture and Commitment: The New Relationship Between the Generations in the 1970s.* New York: Doubleday.

Means, B., ed. 1994. *Technology and Education Reform: The Reality Behind the Promise.* San Francisco: Jossey-Bass.

Merrill, D. 1995. *Evaluation of Educational Technology: What Do We Know, and What Can We Know.* May. Washington, D.C.: Rand Corporation.

Michigan Curriculum Framework: Content Standards and Benchmarks. 1995. Lansing: Michigan Department of Education.

Montague, Marjorie. 1990. *Computers, Cognition, and Writing Instruction.* Albany: State University of New York Press.

Moris, Francisco A. 1996. "Semiconductors: The Building Blocks of the Information Revolution." *Monthly Labor Review* 119 (August): 6–17.

National Center for Education Statistics. 1987a. *Digest of Education Statistics.* Washington, D.C.: Government Printing Office.

———. 1987b. *The Condition of Education.* Washington, D.C.: Government Printing Office.

The National Information Infrastructure: Agenda for Action. 15 September 1993. Information Infrastructure Task Force. U.S. Department of Commerce.

Nax, Sanford. 1996. "Education, Skills Called Twenty-First Century Job Musts." *Fresno Bee*, 25 October, C1.

Negroponte, Nicholas. 1995. *Being Digital.* New York: Alfred A. Knopf.

Neuwirth, C., D. S. Kaufer, and C. Geisler. 1984. "What is EPISTLE?" *Computers and Composition* 1(4): 1–2.

Ohmann, R. 1985. "Literacy, Technology, and Monopoly Capitalism." *College English* 47(7): 675–89.

Olson, C. Paul. 1987. "Who Computes?" *Critical Pedagogy and Cultural Power.* Ed. David Livingstone. South Hadley, Mass.: Bergin and Garvey. 179–204.

"Open Up Your Child's Mind." 1997. Advertisement. *HomePC*, September, 109.

Oppel, Shelby. 1997. "Computer Lab Offers Escape from Poverty." *St. Petersburg Times*, 17 September, 3B.

Oppenheimer, Todd. 1997. "The Computer Delusion." *Atlantic Monthly*, 280(1): 45–62.

Perkins, D., J. Schwartz, M. West, M. Wiske, eds. 1995. *Software Goes to School: Teaching for Understanding with New Technologies.* New York: Oxford University Press.

Phelps, Alan. 1997. "PC Parenting: Using the Home Computer for Quality Education." *Computing for Kids,* summer, 4–7.

Pincus, Fred. 1984. "Students Being Groomed for Jobs That Won't Exist." *Guardian,* 9 May, 7.

"President Clinton Sends 1999 Education Budget to Congress." March 1998. *Community Update* 55. Washington, D.C.: Department of Education.

Public Law 102-73, the National Literacy Act of 1991. House of Representatives Bill 751. 25 July.

Reid, Stephen, and Gilbert Findlay. 1986. "Writer's Workbench Analysis of Holistically Scored Essays." *Computers and Composition* 3(2): 6–32.

"Renewing the Commitment to a Public Interest Telecommunications Policy." 1994. *Communications of the ACM* 37(1): 106–8.

"Retail Trade—Sales by Kind of Business." 1994. Table #1258. U.S. Bureau of the Census, Current Business Reports, Combined Annual and Revised Monthly Retail Trade, January 1985–December 1994, BR/94-RV. <http://www.census.gov/statab/freq>.

Rheingold, H. 1993. *The Virtual Community: Homesteading on the Electronic Frontier.* Reading, Mass.: Addison-Wesley.

Riess, Donna, Dickie Selfe, and Aart Young. 1998. *Electronic Communication Across the Curriculum.* Urbana, Ill.: National Council of Teachers of English.

Roberts, E., ed. 1993. *Computers and Society.* New York: Van Nostrand Reinholt.

Rodrigues, Dawn. 1985. "Computers and Basic Writers." *College Composition and Communication* 36(3): 336–39.

Rodrigues, Raymond J., and Dawn W. Rodrigues. 1984. "Computer-Based Invention: Its Place and Potential." *College Composition and Communication* 35(1): 78–87.

Romero, Mercado, and Vazquez-Faria. 1987. "Students of Limited English Proficiency." *Educators' Handbook: A Research Perspective.* Ed. Virginia Richardson Koehler. White Plains, N.Y.: Longman. 348–69.

Rose, Mike. 1989. *Lives on the Boundary: The Struggles and Achievements of America's Underprepared.* New York: Free Press.

Rothstein, Edward. 1997. "Technology: Connections." *New York Times,* 7 July, D3.

Sanders, Barry. 1995. *A is for Ox: The Collapse of Literacy and the Rise of Violence in an Electronic Age.* New York: Vintage Books.

Schrage, Michael. 1990. *Shared Minds: The New Technologies of Collaboration.* New York: Random House.

Schuler, Douglas. 1994. "Community Networks: Building a New Participatory Medium." *Communications of the ACM* 37(1): 39–51.

Schwartz, Helen, and Lillian S. Bridwell. 1984. "A Selected Bibliography on Computers in Composition." *College Composition and Communication* 35(1): 71–77.

Selber, Stuart A., ed. 1997. *Computers and Technical Communication: Pedagogical and Programmatic Perspectives.* Greenwich, Conn.: Ablex.

Selfe, Cynthia L. 1999. "Technology and Literacy: A Story about the Perils of Not Paying Attention." *College Composition and Communication* 50(3): 411–36.

Selfe, Cynthia L., and S. Hilligoss. 1994. *Literacy and Computers: The Complications of Teaching and Learning with Technology.* New York: Modern Language Association.

Selfe, Cynthia, Dawn Rodrigues, and William Oates. 1989. *Computers in English and the Language Arts: The Challenge of Teacher Education.* Urbana, Ill.: National Council of Teachers of English.

Selfe, Cynthia L., and Richard J. Selfe. 1994. "The Politics of the Interface: Power and Its Exercise in Electronic Contact Zones." *College Composition and Communication* 45(4): 480–504.

Selfe, Cynthia L., and Billie J. Wahlstrom. 1983. "The Benevolent Beast: Computer-Assisted Instruction for the Teaching of Writing." *Writing Instructor* 2 (summer): 183–92.

———. 1986. "An Emerging Rhetoric of Collaboration: Computers, Collaboration, and the Composing Process." *Collegiate Microcomputer* 4(4): 289–95.

Selfe, Richard J. 1997. "Critical Technical Literacy Practices in and Around Technology-Rich Communications Facilities." Ph.D. diss., Michigan Technological University, Houghton.

Sheingold, Karen, L. M. W. Martin, and M. W. Endreweit. 1987. "Preparing Urban Teachers for the Technological Future." *Mirrors of the Mind: Patterns of Experience in Educational Computing.* Ed. Roy D. Pea and Karen Sheingold. Norwood, N.J.: Ablex. 67–85.

Shor, Ira. 1987. *Critical Teaching and Everyday Life.* Chicago: University of Chicago Press.

Silberman, Steve. 1994. "We're Teen, We're Queer, and We've Got E-Mail." *Wired* 2(11).

Skubikowski, Kathleen, and John Elder. 1990. "Computers and the Social Contexts of Writing." *Computers and Community: Teaching Composition in the Twenty-First Century.* Ed. C. Handa. Portsmouth, N.H.: Boynton/Cook Heinemann. 89–105.

"Small Computers, Small Hands." 1997. *HomePC*, September, 174.

Snow, C. P. 1964. *The Two Cultures and a Second Look.* Cambridge: Cambridge University Press.

Southwell, Michael G. 1983. "Computer-Assisted Instruction in Composition at

Works Cited 175

York College/CUNY: Composition for Basic Writing Students." *Writing Instructor* 2 (summer): 165–72.

Sproull, Lee, and Sara Kiesler. 1991a. *Connections: New Ways of Working Within the Networked Organization.* Cambridge: MIT Press.

———. 1991b. "Computers, Networks, and Work." *Scientific American* September, 116–23.

Standards for the English Language Arts. 1996. Newark, Del., and Urbana, Ill.: International Reading Association and the National Council of Teachers of English.

Stoll, Clifford. 1995. *Silicon Snake Oil: Second Thoughts on the Information Highway.* New York: Doubleday.

Stonier, Tom. 1983. *The Wealth of Information: A Profile of the Post Industrial Economy.* London: Methuen.

Street, Brian V. 1995. *Social Literacies: Critical Approaches to Literacy in Development, Ethnography, and Education.* London: Longman.

Strickland, James. 1997. *From Disk to Hard Copy: Teaching Writing with Computers.* Portsmouth, N.H.: Boynton/Cook Heinemann.

Strong, L. A. 1989. "The Best Kids They Have." *Educational Leadership* 46(5): 2.

Stuckey, Elspeth. 1991. *The Violence of Literacy.* Portsmouth, N.H.: Boynton/Cook Heinemann.

Sudol, Ronald A. 1985. "Applied Word Processing: Notes on Authority, Responsibility, and Revision in a Workshop Model." *College Composition and Communication* 36(3): 331–35.

Sullivan, Patricia, and Jennie Dautermann. 1996. *Electronic Literacies in the Workplace: Technologies of Writing.* Urbana, Ill., and Houghton, Mich.: National Council of Teachers of English and Computers and Composition Press.

Sweet, Michael. 1997. "Macs or PCs? Which System Is Right for Your Kids?" *Computing for Kids,* summer, 33–34.

Talbot, S. 1995. *The Future Does Not Compute: Transcending the Machine in Our Midst.* Sebastopol, Calif.: O'Reilly and Associates.

Tannenbaum, A. S. 1996. *Computer Networks.* 3d ed. Upper Saddle River, N.J.: Prentice Hall PTR.

"Tearing U.S. Apart, Part 7: Computers." 1996. *Atlanta Journal and Constitution,* 27 July, 10A.

Toffler, Alvin. 1970. *Future Shock.* New York: Random House.

———. 1980. *The Third Wave.* New York: Morrow.

Trends Tables: Computers and Peripherals (SIC 3571). U.S. Department of Commerce, Bureau of the Census, International Trade Administration. <http://www.ita.doc.gov/industry/otea/usito98/tables/357a.txt>

Turkle, Sherry. 1995. *Turkle's Life on the Screen: Identity in the Age of the Internet.* New York: Simon and Schuster.

Warnke, Jacqueline. 1996. "Computer Manufacturing: Change and Competition." *Monthly Labor Review* 119 (August): 18–29.

Watson, Russell. 1995. "When Words Are the Best Weapon." *Newsweek*, 27 February, 36–40.

Weiser, Mark. 1991. "The Computer for the Twenty-First Century." *Scientific American*, July, 94–104.

Wheelock, A., and G. Dorman. 1989. *Before It's Too Late*. Boston: Massachusetts Advocacy Commission.

"Why Settle for the Moon?" 1997. Advertisement. *HomePC*, September, 115.

Wilson, David L., ed. 1993. "Private Liberal Arts College Found to Lag in Internet Access and Sophisticated Computers." *Chronicle of Higher Education*, 15 December, A17.

Winner, Langdon. 1986. "Mythinformation." *The Whale and the Reactor: A Search for Limits in an Age of High Technology*. Chicago: University of Chicago Press. 98–117.

Wiser, James L. 1990. "Technological Consciousness and the Modern Understanding of the Good Life." *From Artifact to Habitat: Studies in the Critical Engagement of Technology*. Bethlehem, Penn.: Lehigh University Press. 60–73.

Wresch, William. 1982. "Computers in English Class: Finally Beyond Grammar and Spelling." *College English* 44:483–90.

Zimmer, JoAnn. 1985. "The Continuing Challenge: Computers and Writing." *Computers and Composition* 2(3): 4–6.

Zuboff, S. 1988. *In the Age of the Smart Machine: The Future of Work and Power*. New York: Basic Books.

Index

Gilbert, S. W., 71

Global Information Infrastructure
(GII), 51, 97, 118, 119, 123; expansion of, 55–57; and international
effects of growth in computer industry, 93–96; and introduction of Technology Literacy Challenge, 57–61

Goals 2000: Educate America Act (HR
1804), 75–76, 78

Gomez, Mary Louise, 65, 66, 72, 73

Goodman, William, 8, 90, 94, 96

good parent/providing parent narrative:
and technological literacy, 104–8

Gore, Albert, 47, 50, 77, 97, 118, 120;
and education, in ideology of technological literacy, 122; and GII, 55, 56,
93; and introduction of Technology
Literacy Challenge, 59–60

government. See Clinton, Bill; Gore,
Albert; Riley, Richard

Graff, Harvey, 18, 19, 23, 134, 135,
136, 148, 160

Green, Kenneth, 83–84

Griffin, Peg, 65, 66

*Gutenberg Elegies: The Fate of Reading
in an Electronic Age* (Birkert), 25,
26; as negative representation of
technology, 32, 34–36

Gutenberg Galaxy (McLuhan), 25, 26

Handa, Carolyn, 8

Hansen, Craig J., 14, 84

Haraway, Donna, 147

Hardy, H. E., 48

Harris, Jeannette, 69

Hawisher, Gail E., 8, 10, 49, 70, 84,
108, 143

Heidegger, Martin, 116; on technology,
140–42

Herrmann, Andrea, 70

Hilligoss, S., 8, 84

Hoffman, Donna L., 67

Hohmann, Charles, 98

Holdstein, Deborah, 69

Holstrom, David, 133

HomePC, 100, 103; and good par-
ent/providing parent narrative, 105–

8; and parents as agents for technological literacy, 110–12

human resources development: and
NII and GII, 61–63

ideology: naturalization of systems of,
124–28; role of, in technological literacy, 114–15, 130

IMF. See International Monetary Fund

Improving America's School Act, 62

information retrieval: growth in, 90

Intel, 88

International Federation of Teachers of
English, 159

International Monetary Fund (IMF), 45

International Reading Association, 159

International Telecommunications
Union, 50

Internet, 12; and development of computer networks, 47–49; growth of,
87. See also networks, computer

Jabs, Carolyn, 103, 109

Jackson, Cheryl: on good parent/pro-
viding parent narrative, 104–5

Jessup, Emily, 66

Jobst, John, 69

Johnson-Eilola, Johndan, 14

Jones, Robert, 84

Kiesler, Sara, 48, 121

King, B., 69

Kinkead, Joyce, 69

Klem, Elizabeth, 70, 71

knowledges, situated: and paying attention to literacy-technology link, 146–
48; as sites for critical technological
literacy development, 148–59

Kobler, Ron, 101–2

Landow, George P., 84

Lanham, Richard, 121

Latour, Bruno, 9, 21, 144–45

LeBlanc, Paul, 8, 49, 69, 70, 84

libraries: as site for critical technological literacy development, 157–58

Life on the Screen (Turkle), 25

technology: American specialization in, 47; changing nature of, 3–5; and democracy, in ideology of technological literacy, 116–19; dichotomous representations of, 36–39; and education, in ideology of technological literacy, 119–23; expansion of, and economic expansion, 49–51; Heidegger on, 140–42; and literacy, 133–34; negative representations of, 32–36; positive representations of, 26–32; and science, in ideology of technological literacy, 115–16. *See also* computer industry; computers

Technology Initiative: and development of NII, 51–55. *See also* National Information Infrastructure

Technology Literacy Challenge, 5–7, 21–24, 43–44, 73, 130, 133, 161; and definitions of technological literacy, 10–15; funding for, 15–17, 81–82; introduction of, 59–60, 62; and literacy education as political act, 137–39; and myth of literacy, 134–37; negative effects of, 8–9; positive effects of, 7–8; role of educators in, 9–10, 142–44; social costs of, 20–21. *See also* literacy, technological

Telecommunications Act, 59, 62

Telecommunications Policy Roundtable, 53–54

Third Wave, The (Toffler), 47

Thurlow, Eric, 98

Toffler, Alvin, 50

trade, 117; liberalized international, 46–47

unemployment, 45. *See also* employment

"Universal Service Does Matter" (Glaser), 157

values, 123; and technological literacy, 12–15. *See also* belief systems

Virtual Community (Rheingold), 25, 26; as positive representation of technology, 28, 30–32

Wageman, J., 69

Wahlstrom, Billie J., 68, 70

Warnke, Jacqueline, 8, 88, 90

Watson, Russell, 57

Weiser, Mark, 159–60

"We're Teen, We're Queer, and We've Got E-Mail" (Selber), 157

Wiser, James, 116

word processing: and English teachers' use of computers in the classroom, 70

World Wide Web (WWW), 12. *See also* networks, computer

Wresch, William, 68

Writing Center Journal, 84

Wysocki, Anne, 153

Young, Art, 84

Zimmer, JoAnn, 69

Zuboff, S., 14

CYNTHIA L. SELFE is a professor of humanities in the Humanities Department at Michigan Technological University. She has chaired the Conference on College Composition and Communication and the College Section of the National Council of Teachers of English. In 1996, she was awarded the EDUCOM Medal for innovative computer use in higher education. The author of numerous articles and books on computers, she is the founder (with Kathleen Kiefer) and coeditor (with Gail Hawisher) of *Computers and Composition: An International Journal for Teachers of Writing.*